TRANSFORMING
WORSHIP

TRANSFORMING
WORSHIP

Timothy L. Carson

CHALICE
PRESS
ST. LOUIS, MISSOURI

Bible quotations, unless otherwise marked, are from the *New Revised Standard Version Bible*, copyright 1989, Division of Christian Education of the National Council of the Churches of Christ in the United States of America. Used by permission. All rights reserved.

Cover art: Stained-glass window, St. Theresa's, Phoenix, Arizona; photograph
        © The Crosiers
Cover and interior design: Elizabeth Wright
Art direction: Elizabeth Wright

This book is printed on acid-free, recycled paper.

Visit Chalice Press on the World Wide Web at
www.chalicepress.com

10 9 8 7 6 5 4 3 2 1   03 04 05   06   07   08

Library of Congress Cataloging–in–Publication Data

Carson, Timothy L.
   Transforming worship / Timothy Carson.
      p. cm.
Includes bibliographical references.
   ISBN 0-8272-3642-5 (alk. paper)
   1. Public worship. I. Title.
   BV15.C39 2003
   264—dc21
                                        2003001251

For my parents, Thelma and George,
my first teachers of worship

Contents

Acknowledgments

For their insights into Christian origins, church history, and ecumenics, I am indebted to Dr. Stephen Patterson, professor of New Testament, Eden Theological Seminary, St. Louis, Missouri; Dr. James Duke, professor of church history, Brite Divinity School, Fort Worth, Texas; and Dr. Michael Kinnamon, professor of mission and peace, Eden Theological Seminary, St. Louis, Missouri.

The Association of Disciples Musicians allowed me to present bits and pieces of this work at their 2001 national workshop. The ingredients of the manuscript were still brewing at that time, and for their attentiveness and encouragement, I am thankful.

I would also like to thank a coterie of worship innovators and practitioners, two of whom are Robert Ferre of the St. Louis Labyrinth Project and Gary Duncan of the Sacred Spaces ministry of St. Andrews Christian Church of Olathe, Kansas.

Most of all, I would like to pay tribute to the many persons of faith who are doing extraordinary worship work in congregations. You often serve in typical settings that could seem unremarkable. I know better. Your efforts are often fraught with passion, creativity, and faithfulness, and this in the face of unusual challenges. You are the ones who so often inspire, move, and educate me. From the bottom of my heart, thank you.

Editorial Note

The author and editor decided that all sources would be listed in one location at the end of the manuscript without notating them specifically throughout. This choice was made in order to protect the conversational tone of the book while also giving credit where credit is due.

Introduction

For us to hear that the twentieth century contained a tremendous ferment in worship is like saying that chocolate ice cream and pecan pie are sweet; it's true enough, but obvious. It is also apparent that liturgical life in the church has not been the only thing changing. Who doesn't know that every facet of life has been subjected to change of a quantum order? This is not news. Tell us something we don't know.

On the other hand, we incline toward grandiosity. Surely, we tell ourselves, we are going where no one has ever gone before. To what could we possibly compare the dramatic change of our own era? Well, communion of saints, humor us. We're not as arrogant or uninformed as we might seem. We have it at least half-right.

What we understand correctly is that the immediate past century may indeed take the gold cup for being the historical period of the greatest rapidity, volume, and complexity of change. People of great longevity who lived for a hundred years between 1900 and 2000 witnessed an almost unbelievable breadth of change. Many of them sat in our pews. They were the ones who finally stopped saying, "Now I've seen it all."

What we misunderstand, however, is that earlier centuries of Christians faced equally shocking and shaking developments. We forget the innovative and sometimes heroic ways in which they adapted and often flourished. By remembering, we can avoid the inclination toward either excessive self-congratulation or undue self-pity.

The same is also true of liturgical reform, renewal, and innovation. We are not the first to engage in reform, revision, and innovation. We are not the first to witness the cultural terrain shift around us. We are not the first to experience a tension between the generations, yet our time does present a peculiar challenge for worship. Sailing these seas does require special attention to particular protruding or concealed hazards.

As to Christians of every time, faithfulness to the gospel calls us to respond to the challenges presented to us.

As we walk and converse together through the following pages, let us think about how we can cocreate a worship that is truly transforming—for individual persons and for our communities of faith. How is faithful worship the same as or different from that of Christians in the first generation, or of the Reformation, or among the founders of our distinctive movements? How have our inherited traditions provided either helpful foundations or difficult hindrances in joining the new movement of the Spirit? In what ways can we balance form with freedom and enduring truths with new ways of communication and perception?

If the heart of worship requires lifting the heart to glorify God, the very lifeblood of the church is at stake. If future generations of Christians will remember us for anything, it will be for the same reasons that we remember past saints: determination to honor God in everything we do, fearlessness in finding the way through uncharted waters, and the glad songs of a people who have again found the peace that passes understanding.

CHAPTER ONE

From Simple to Complex

The Expansion of the Liturgy

Day by day, as they spent much time together in the temple, they broke bread at home and ate their food with glad and generous hearts, praising God and having the goodwill of all the people.

ACTS 2:46–47

Christian worship has always ricocheted between complexity and simplicity. In addition, a tension between form and freedom has ensured the moving, changing, and reforming of liturgical practices. Whenever dynamic movement has slowed for a sustained period of time, a reform or reform movement has emerged to either innovate or replace what went before. In the same way that the main channel of a river produces its own countercurrents, so dominant forms of worship eventually do the same; they foster their own successors and alternatives.

Movements of renewal often resemble one another in important ways and contain many of the same reforming elements: a search for the essentials; new doses of spirit injected into old forms; and key leaders who hold hope in their hearts and dreams for a brighter day. The predictable result of these movements is that some practices are discarded as new traditions replace them. More often, a new synthesis is created from combining both.

The process that is created by this dynamic interchange is glacierlike in its appearance. It is like water freezing and expanding until climate shifts finally bring about its warming, melting, and contracting. What is added in one era may melt away in the next or melt and refreeze in another form. Yet throughout, it remains water. Such is the perennial nature of tradition with its continuity and flux.

The origins of Christian worship remain obscure. We are certain, however, that those origins were preceded by the worship practices that already existed in the time of Jesus. They provided the context for his ministry. What we know about this historically, however, remains fairly limited.

The liturgical milieu of first-century Israel most obviously included the rites of the Jerusalem temple. From liturgical material embedded in such scriptures as the Psalms, we have a partial written record of early temple practices. Archaeology and descriptions of physical structure give insight into worship space and its use. Aside from that, though, little is known about the temple's actual degree of influence on early Christians.

Although Jews technically worshiped in only one place, the temple, early Christians were often divided over its significance. We are aware of Jesus' harsh critique of temple practices, that tribute for Rome was collected at the temple site, and that priests collaborated in doing so. However, this kind of involvement of Jesus with the temple does not provide us with insights into worship nearly as much as it does with stories of conflict with authority and competing visions of the nature of God. In the end, the worship practices of the temple, though important, do not shed great light on the emergence of worship in the earliest Christian communities.

Much of what we do know about either synagogue worship or Christian worship of the first generation is gleaned from a later period, the time following the destruction of the temple in 70 C.E. For both Jews and Christians, their worship outside of temple practice would not be regularized until later. From that later vantage point, we deduce practices that existed or were beginning to exist earlier. In the earliest record, we do not have extensive descriptions of what that worship was like.

The ministry of Jesus was primarily focused in the local communities of Galilean villages, homes, and synagogues.

We do know that early Christians gathered in homes. We know they ate together, sang songs, and talked about Jesus. From our understandings of social interaction in the first century, we may suppose that the traditional social meal, a primary means of social formation for both pagans and Hellenized Jews, provided form for such Christian gatherings. We also know that they baptized one another, though it is not perfectly clear how or when.

The role of the common meal was critical to the formation of the Christian communities and their emerging worship. As Christians began to develop their life more liturgically, it was often from the meal that they launched. Distinctive Christian practices such as the Lord's supper or foot washing matured in these intimate community meals. In addition to the common meals, there was also a second great influence, that of the synagogue service.

Although information about synagogue life in the first century is quite partial, we do know from both Matthew and John that Christians at the end of the first century were being asked to leave the synagogue. Following the destruction of the temple and its cataclysmic aftermath in 70 C.E., Jewish and Jewish Christian communities became increasingly estranged and separate. The implication is that before the destruction of the temple the synagogue would have been a place of worship for both Jews and Jewish Christians. In the same way that Jesus frequented the synagogue, so the first generation Jesus movement, itself a Jewish sect, observed the Sabbath. Christians would have participated in both synagogue services and common meals.

Slowly, in a process that eventually separated the Jesus movement from its worship roots, the Christians moved to their own unique worship gatherings. To say that the Christians were separated from Jewish communities of worship is not to say, however, that the influences of synagogue worship disappeared. Quite to the contrary, the form and contents of the synagogue service no doubt provided a foundation on which Christian worship grew. Although it would be too simple to say that Christians simply appropriated the synagogue service for their own purposes, we could say that the synagogue worship remained a strong influence on them. What can we clearly say about synagogue services as they are known from a later period, after the destruction of the temple?

The synagogue service included the recitation of the Shema, psalms, and prayers (the Eighteen Benedictions); readings from Torah and the Prophets; and an exposition on those scriptures. We are provided a portrait that includes some of the elements of a typical service in the story of Jesus' visiting the synagogue in Nazareth on the Sabbath (Luke 4). As was the custom, he rose to read from the scripture and then sat to expound on it. This depiction of typical synagogue worship provides us with some of the typical patterns that would become normative for Jewish Christian worship.

As Christian practice reflected much of the synagogue service form and content, it also undoubtedly reflected a distinctive Christian theology: teaching and proclamation were offered; letters from Christian witnesses were read; and Christian songs and hymns were sung. Many of these early Christian hymns are lodged in letters and tracts from the early Christian communities. The hymn to the Logos in John 1, the Redeemer hymn in Philippians 2, and the paean to the Lamb in Revelation 5 are remarkable examples.

As the practices and influences of the common meal and the synagogue service were joined together in complex ways, they created the beginnings of a worship that would later evolve into a twofold reality of word and sacrament.

Other elements of Christian worship in the earliest tradition are found in the Pauline correspondence. The liturgical fragments that are discovered there, however, are most often discovered as part of a narrative backdrop for some cultural or religious conflict in the Hellenistic milieu. For example, the issue of the manifestation and appropriate use of spiritual gifts in the gathered community of worship may be more the result of a pervasive encounter with enthusiasts from mystery religions and cults who have converted to Christianity (1 Cor. 12) than with an attempt to develop a systematic theology of the Holy Spirit. However, a repository of teaching on the Spirit is present nonetheless. Teaching about the Lord's table may have arisen more directly as an attempt to address abuses and conflicts surrounding Greco-Roman meal practices and social stratification (1 Cor. 11) than to outline a theology of communion, but the by-product of that struggle is the outline of the liturgical sharing of an entire meal to commemorate Jesus. In both these cases, the happy result of situational letters to unhappy congregations is coincidental information about first-century worship practices. Because the apostle Paul both received a tradition of the Lord's supper and then clarified its theology and practice in a particular context of conflict, a new and relevant word was passed on to a community of faith grounded in a particular time and place. That this powerful combination finally became part of the canon should not be lost on us; an older tradition and a newer one often join to create a new synthesis for a new context.

Christian worship has always been shaped by the traditions that preceded it and the cultural forms and practices in which the community lived. For example, the Didache, the early extrabiblical work, provided doctrinal teaching in the form of a catechism, teaching liturgical practices that had become normative for their community. This includes such things as the Lord's Prayer, baptism, and a core of traditional practices and beliefs that were gathered together in a vessel that could be passed from one generation to the next. However, because the Didache not only accumulated the history of its predecessors but also taught it to a new generation of believers, it passed on a re-presented form and content to its descendants. The consequence of this process of transmission was that the tradition was expanded through its formalization.

In one of our congregation's treasured Christmas traditions, we celebrate the nativity through carols, drama, and readings. Practically every year we add one more facet to the expanding tradition. Over time, each of these new additions comes to be seen as indispensable. Every part earns its own treasured place and is anticipated from year to year. If something is deleted by intent or accident, there is sure to be loud wailing and lamentation, Rachel weeping for her children, for they are no more!

Many of the additions to the liturgy and the teaching about it were directed toward the already existing worshiping community. Those persons were, of course, the primary concern of Christian teaching. However, there was also a world to engage, one in which the church lived and related. The way in which Christians did that—related to their world and made the case for their faith—also became part of its tradition and liturgy. The *why* of its practices became part of *the tradition itself*. A case in point is Justin Martyr.

Justin Martyr was born in Samaria and moved to Ephesus at the beginning of the second century. He then moved to Rome, where he taught and was eventually martyred in 165 C.E. Initially a philosopher, he was converted to Christian teaching and became a primary spokesperson for the faith. Lest we fool ourselves into thinking that "seeker-sensitive" teaching and worship is something new and unique, Justin was one of the early apologists, one who bridged Christian and non-Christian worlds with words. No less remarkable for us is that his words were penned a mere hundred years after the apostle Paul had written the earliest of his letters.

In Justin's *First Apology,* he makes an eloquent case for Christianity; and in the last seven chapters, he provides an extensive description of Christian worship in the mid-second century. Because he was motivated by the desire to make Christian thought and practice clear to outsiders and to quell unfounded rumors, his writing was simple and comprehensive. His explanation accompanies description.

This includes an account of how Christians met together in one place; celebrated on the Lord's Day (the first day of creation and the day of resurrection); shared a service of the Word, which would roughly parallel the Jewish synagogue service but also include readings from the apostles (portions of what we call our New Testament before those writings were canonized); listened to discourse on those readings delivered from the cathedra (the teacher's chair); and stood for common prayer.

There is some implication that the unbaptized were dismissed from the assembly before the service of the believers that would include the Lord's Prayer, but this is not as certain in Justin as it is in later writings. After the exchange of a holy kiss (men with men, women with women), bread and water mingled with wine were presented to the presider, who offered the communion prayer extemporaneously. The prayer included such things as a thanksgiving to God for grace, the creation of the world, Christ, and the salvation of humanity. Words of institution were offered, including the words, "This is my body, do this in remembrance of me," and likewise for the cup, saying, "This is my blood." Then the deacons administered the bread and wine to the assembly and carried it off to those who were unable to be present. The Lord's table was a thanksgiving, a remembrance, a sign of the unity of the faithful, and a recognition of the presence of Christ through the Holy Spirit.

Interestingly, Justin insists that no persons were to take the holy food unless they embraced the truth of Christian teaching and were baptized. The communion would be an expression of the faith already embraced. As Justin was an apologist for the faith to a surrounding culture of unbelief, it is understandable that theological assent would be tied closely to ritual practice.

What is clear in both his teaching about worship and his description of the practice of worship is that Justin maintained a bifocal gaze on the believing community and those whom he engaged outside of it. His sharp clarifications existed to form the faith of one already captured by the gospel message and also to inspire the intellectual underpinnings of a seeker's nascent faith. This pastoral teaching and apologetic discourse were compiled into a divine office that served as a sufficient voice for the worship of the people of God. Because it strove to be all-embracing, Justin's liturgy and teaching about it codified the tradition in ever-expanding ways.

If Justin's primary emphasis was to relate the gospel to the world, Hippolytus, bishop of Rome at the close of the second century, gave himself to defending the tradition from the assault of perceived heretics. As opposed to his apologist predecessor, Hippolytus inherited a time of terrible doctrinal dissension, internal division, and the rise and influence of movements that were understood to be heretical. His challenge, therefore, was to make the case for a theologically sound form of worship. His manual, *Apostolic Tradition,* was written sometime after 217 C.E. and is an outstanding repository of information about primary models of liturgy known and used at the close of the second and beginning of the third centuries.

Hippolytus passed on a liturgical form and content that was very similar to Justin's; it included a service of Word and table. However, the role of bishop received much greater emphasis. Above all, in that time of competing theological voices, sources of ecclesial authority needed clear identification as well as strong endorsement.

In his eucharistic service, there are no fixed liturgical fragments, and though he provides an example of a eucharistic prayer, the celebrant is allowed to pray extemporaneously. The prayer includes the exaltation of the Logos, the remembrance, and what appears to be an invocation of the Holy Spirit. Whereas the place and participation of the catechumens might be hazy in Justin, they are not in Hippolytus; it is after confirmation and baptism that initiates are brought into the believers' service, share the Lord's Prayer, and participate in the communion service.

The bishop himself, after breaking the bread, administered it to the people, saying, "The bread of heaven." Then the presbyters administered the wine, saying, "In God the Father Almighty." Then the communicants responded to the reception of each by saying, "Amen"—affirming the faith at the very moment of partaking.

To read Hippolytus is to find not an elaborately embroidered liturgy, but rather, a clearly delineated protocol for the enactment of worship. The description of how and by whom the liturgy is offered is perhaps his greatest contribution. One cannot leave Hippolytus without taking away a strong sense of the emerging forms of ministry. Worship leadership was not to be determined or organized in a careless or haphazard way. In fact, its ecclesiology—the community's understanding of the nature of church—shaped the ways it lived out the gospel in its worship life. The bishop and the presbyters all had their respective places within the work of the whole people of God. In addition, all this was wrapped around the twofold pattern of Word and table.

Justin Martyr and Hippolytus provided a clear sense of the basic form, content, and leadership of the expanding Christian liturgy. This included relatively wide latitude of freedom in liturgical particulars. The dawning of the fourth century, on the other hand, presented a very different picture.

A case in point is the Liturgy of Saint James, sometimes referred to as the Jerusalem liturgy, which was known and practiced by the fourth century. By its era, we find considerable formation not only of a fixed order of service but also of exceedingly defined and crystallized contents. This included prescribed responses, elaborate rubrics, and a highly structured order. Although it had not reached the place of the Roman Mass in terms of its structure and ornamentation, there was an extensive and highly stylized ritual. Like a snowball rolling downhill, it had, over time, accumulated a wide liturgical girth, and the process would continue. The church's liturgy would continue to add and refine as it went. On the one hand, it served as a repository of tradition. On the other hand, it continued to adapt to its particular theological, cultural, and political contexts.

In a complex and often uneven process of development, the liturgy moved from its origins in the common meal and influences of the synagogue service toward a more elaborate and prescribed ritual. This trajectory of the developing liturgy eventually led to a complexity that would, in part, contribute to a revolution in the West.

This dramatic change was driven by a powerful social ferment, theological reforms, the emergence of the Enlightenment, and the rise of pietism and revivalistic religion. Significant liturgical shifts were about to shake the church's foundations for centuries to come. Some questioned if the church could survive it, or if it would ever be the same again. It was the right question.

CHAPTER TWO

From Complex to Simple
The Contraction of the Liturgy

"With what shall I come before the LORD,
and bow myself before God on high?
Shall I come before him with burnt offerings,
with calves a year old?
Will the LORD *be pleased with thousands of rams,*
with ten thousands of rivers of oil?"

MICAH 6:6–7A

Such names as Luther, Zwingli, Calvin, and Knox are all affiliated with not only theological and ecclesial moves but also *liturgical* ones. When the reformations of the sixteenth century moved through a rapidly changing European stage, the most conspicuous locale of change was the liturgy itself. Here the battles of ideas raged and the wars between authorities were waged. The omission of time-honored worship elements,

13

the transfiguring of subtle and not-so-subtle language, and the way in which laity and clergy interacted were reflections of a huge, bubbling ferment.

Worship wars may actually be about worship; people do have legitimate concerns and convictions about the way people worship their God. Just as often, however, these skirmishes reflect a more generalized struggle for power. Because the forms and practices of worship occupy the symbolic center of churchly life, the locale of worship is where power and control are most clearly identified and maintained. It is no wonder that resistance to reform manifests itself so often in the context of *liturgical struggle.*

By the time of Martin Luther and his writings on worship in 1523, the undressing of the liturgical Christmas tree was already in full swing. The tinsel came off first, then the ornaments, the lights, and finally the star. What was left standing in the center of the room was little more than the tree itself. Why?

For the sixteenth-century reformers, their understanding of the nature of church determined their worship reforms. For instance, the critique of the misuse of withholding of communion as a way to enforce doctrinal uniformity led to a change in both the sacrament's shape and frequency. The understanding of the priesthood of all believers related directly to the way clergy and laity would participate in the service and how the liturgy would return to the vernacular language. The rise of hymnody of the people dismantled a two-tier worship participation of actors and spectators. The cry of *sola scriptura* brought the preached word to the forefront of the liturgical stage. Liturgical fragments were, by and large, preserved if they came directly from scripture—though they were certainly not used in their traditional locations.

In terms of Luther's suggested service, the general confession and the *Gloria* both disappeared. The *Kyrie* shrunk from nine strands to three. The three lessons remained, but German hymns were interspersed between them. In the eucharistic service, the offertory was dismantled, and what remained was an invitation to communion followed by the words of institution. Ornament by ornament, the tree was undecorated and redecorated. In reformed quarters, in place after place, the expansion of the liturgy gave way to its own radical contraction. Zwingli was about the same project in Zurich, as was Calvin in Geneva, Knox in Edinburgh, and Bucer in Strasbourg.

It was thoroughgoing, except for the Anglicans, who entered reform through their own unique political ways. Even in their case, however, the liturgy was not left unaffected; the language of sacrifice was omitted from the eucharist.

All this was part and parcel of the radical contracting of the liturgy. It was understood as a form of surgery: a stripping away and purposeful return to essentials.

However, what would happen to the actual worship practices of these children of reform over time? What development and change would take place in the span of only two centuries, between 1550 and 1750? The answer is not unexpected or unusual: the movements of these reformers expanded. In general, the liturgy once again grew, developed, and filled out. Prayer books were issued along with scores of hymnals. Long treatises explained which worship practices were acceptable and not acceptable. Lines of authority were reassembled even as new confessions were developed. Worship once again became tightly prescribed.

What would be the result of this new expansion of not only the churchly structure but also of the liturgy itself? A second wave of reform movements arose among *reformers of the reformers*. The second wave of reformers did not hold great animosity toward the original grandmother from whom grandchildren had moved, Catholicism. They instead contended with their own reforming mothers.

In either case, in the first or second generation of Protestant reformers, the dynamics were the same: They reformed the expanded liturgy by simplifying and reducing it to essentials. To reclaim these essentials they attempted to move back to earlier sources of authority. For these Reformers that meant a return to scripture.

When Free Church movements of the American frontier—so defined by the sense of either free governance or non-prescribed liturgy—jumped behind the traditions of their predecessors, they often modeled a radical simplicity. In addition, broad pan-religious movements such as occurred in the first and second Great Awakenings, added revivalist and pietistic dimensions to regular services of worship.

In contrast to the European churches whose liturgies were transplanted into the American context in relatively intact form, Free Church movements were characterized by the absence of prayer books and printed texts. This inspired announced services that depended on known oral traditions for both hymnody and form. Scripture became the final liturgical authority. The only fixed liturgical pieces enjoying regular places in worship had direct biblical sources, the Lord's Prayer and words of institution being prime examples. Prayer was extemporaneous and not prescribed, including prayer at the Lord's table.

So what would happen liturgically in the American context as the nineteenth century gave way to the twentieth? Powerful streams of influence would emerge and reshape the form and content of worship.

The reforms of the Second Vatican Council brought about liturgical renewal that would reach far beyond the Roman Catholic Church. The century preceding Vatican II already had been filled with Catholic liturgical renewal, especially among the Benedictine communities. In a sense, the liturgical reforms of the Second Council represented the culmination and hastening of a process already in existence. The fact that the renewal of and changes in the liturgy were already happening explains why the liturgical reforms of Vatican II could seem to come so quickly and appear so radical. The way had already been prepared. Theologians not only leapt over and behind the dominant scholastics of the high Middle Ages to the earlier church fathers of the first four centuries but also formed new liturgies and rubrics, embraced vernacular language, welcomed lay involvement, and increased ecumenical breadth. Renewal was also meant to foster creative use of prescribed forms, such as new musical or festive settings of the Sanctus, Kyrie, or Gloria. Protestants of the 1960s and 1970s often took their musical and liturgical cues from their reforming Catholic brothers and sisters. The liturgical life of the Protestant monks of Taizé in France is a notable example.

For Protestants of the first Reformation—Lutherans and Reformed—twentieth-century liturgical renewal often meant recovering their sixteenth-century roots. Liturgical studies of Luther and Calvin rediscovered a eucharistic richness that stood in some contrast to their own worship, which had become dry, formal, and highly rationalistic. On the other side of rationalism and German pietism, there appeared a new, enlivened Reformed eucharistic awareness. Serious biblical scholarship by people such as Joachim Jeremias and Oscar Cullmann only added to the impetus to recapture what had been lost.

The Anglicans were the most highly visible of any of the Protestant liturgical reformers. Both in their writing and practice, the rise of the Anglo-Catholic liturgical scholars and practitioners brought the resurgence of Roman roots in worship. This was reflected not only in the multiplication of symbols and rituals but also in newly remodeled neo-Gothic sanctuaries.

Protestants of the Free Church tradition moved and changed in different ways. For many, the age of industrialization brought about a move from rural to urban life. This social shift provided an unavoidable engagement with other religious cultures. This necessarily included forays into the formalized liturgies and church architecture of these new neighbors. This exposure of Free Church parishioners to their Presbyterian, Lutheran, Congregational, and Episcopal neighbors shaped how they viewed their own tradition—if only by comparison. As seminary education of clergy became increasingly ecumenical in scope, the cross-fertilization between traditions became thoroughgoing.

As Free Church congregations struggled to assimilate in their new urban culture, they often attempted a leap to greater liturgical sophistication. As new sanctuaries were constructed, they followed architectural cues of their Episcopal neighbors; the split chancel with high altar became normative. The churches that were historically known for simplicity, freedom, and revival worship gravitated toward an increasing formality. Many Protestant churches of the 1940s and 1950s became dominated by an Eisenhowerian sense of respectable worship protocol. The worship experiences of nineteenth-century revivalism became institutionalized as a pattern for worship. There would still be an altar call, but now the minister was wearing a clerical robe. The hymnody might still be revivalistic, but the choir's anthem of the day was taken from the classical tradition. Slowly the influences of the new liturgical renewal movement replaced the earlier revivalism. There was a tension between their revivalistic heritage and liturgical renewal, to be sure. For Protestants in the Free Church tradition, this liturgical borrowing all too frequently took place without sufficient historical or theological grounding. The problem persists to this day.

One of the major contributions of the worldwide ecumenical movement of the twentieth century was a developing consensus about the shape of the historic ecumenical liturgy.

Some of the remarkable ecumenical fruit included the *COCU Liturgy*, the result of extended work by the *Consultation on Church Union*, and the *Lima Liturgy*, which was based on the text of *Baptism, Eucharist, and Ministry*. The reception of *Baptism, Eucharist, and Ministry* into the larger church's life signaled a new and thoroughgoing ecumenical theology of liturgy. Its impact on forming the worship consciousness of theologians, pastors, and laity remains unequaled. The Faith and Order

Commission of the World Council of Churches continued to produce compelling worldwide research about the nature of eucharistic patterns of worship.

The ecumenical consensus relied not only on scriptural roots but also, like the second Vatican Council, on the early patristic material. The recovery of Hippolytus and his *Apostolic Tradition,* as well as other anti-Nicaean doctors of the church, added to the clear identification of the simple pattern of Christian worship. This signaled the clear and unequivocal centrality of the eucharist within a full service of Word and table.

Sustained ecumenical work also led to attentiveness to the worship of different cultures. This increasing awareness of the church of the world gave rise to intercession for other parts of the world as well as the crucial link between worship and social justice. The Vancouver Assembly of the World Council of Churches included a remarkable adaptation of the Lima Liturgy to the multicultural expressions of worship and signaled a new phase of liturgical convergence.

This multicultural awareness stands in some contrast to the ways in which European theology is done and expressed. The latter is generally quite discursive and embeds its important theological convictions in print-culture liturgies; the normative ecumenical consensus often came to resemble a theological treatise dressed for worship. That would create a later problem for any church that desired to claim the ecumenical consensus while also moving beyond print-culture worship. On the other hand, different streams within the ecumenical movement have emphasized such things as music and symbol—precisely because they transcend differences and cut through the barriers of language, culture, and confession.

All these recent movements of liturgical reform and renewal have, in one way or another, created our present worship milieu. As always, this leaves faithful Christians with hard questions about their future as worshiping communities of faith. They are not new questions, as we have seen, but they remain urgent ones. The liturgy is always developing and expanding, but also reforming, changing, seeking essentials, and contracting.

How shall we dance between complexity and simplicity now? In our context, do we find ourselves at the apex of expansion or in a movement toward contraction? What does it mean for serious Christians to engage with their origins, core values, and tradition and yet reach to modern culture as apologists? How might unity be fostered within theological and liturgical form? How does a community both form and re-form at the same time? Is it possible to remain faithful in receiving, modifying, and passing on ancient or modern tradition?

What does it mean to be a worshiping community in our present context, living somewhere between the Enlightenment and what comes after it? How can religious persons both critique and apply the all-determining technology that is so characteristic of our era? What expansion or contraction is necessary now? Why and in what ways?

CHAPTER THREE

Postmodern Dance

Worship in the New World

Likewise the Spirit helps us in our weakness; for we do not know how to pray as we ought, but that very Spirit intercedes with sighs too deep for words.

ROMANS 8:26

A leisurely stroll through our present culture reveals an astounding array of radically divergent lifestyles, worldviews, art forms, religious movements, ethnic subcultures, and political persuasions. Even the most heterogeneous community is now surrounded by places, people, and practices it has never personally witnessed. The world has invaded—electronically—and not even the most remote havens of isolation are capable of shielding their inhabitants from the onslaught. Satellite transmissions bring instantaneous news from across the planet to every living room. Young people surf the Internet and chat with peers from every country under the sun. Cell phones provide an ever-present connection that both serves and constrains their users. College students travel abroad as a matter of course, exploring other cultures in the first person. Musical groups create eclectic combinations of the traditional and the nouveau that seem perfectly natural. We're not in Kansas anymore, Toto. No, we're not.

On the religious front, the same realities exist. Some people clamor for ancient things that provide the mystery and awe that the rest of their lives lack. Others seek one injection after another of high-voltage stimuli that make colors dance on the inside of their closed eyelids. Cyberspirituality supplies the discriminating religious shopper with every vintage and brand under the sun, all without the messy necessity of being in the actual presence of other human beings. Hundreds of chat rooms serve up everything from low-calorie inspirations to the prayer rooms of people hunched over their laptops, receiving and replying to e-prayer requests.

In spite of all this quantum change, the tried-and-true religious traditions keep on keeping on, often in a dizzying descent into oblivion, but not always. Surprisingly, tenacious congregations who know who they are and why they exist not only survive but also thrive.

There is also the great silence. It is the deep breathing of skeptic observers who don't believe a word of it for a minute. They sit, bemused on the sidelines, watching with wide-open eyes, or not watching at all. Enough scandals have come and gone to dismiss any or all of it with ease. Their friends have slipped in and out of megachurches enough times that the watchers just look askance at the little empires. Too many cable preachers and their flocks are just plain embarrassing Even if I'm not bowling alone, I may be worshiping alone, and I don't anticipate that changing anytime soon.

Of course, many are not about to abandon the search for a community of faith in which they may worship and serve. Whether the current morass leads them to incense or rocking for Jesus or both, it's clear that the fault lines have shifted. Is it any wonder that in this time of unprecedented change the proverbial pillars should be shaking? Which direction should we go? Or should we move at all, lest the fragile house of cards comes tumbling down?

There is perhaps no more ambiguous word today than *postmodern*. Yet even in its fuzziness, it captures the essence of what we are in and that to which we are heading. It is the "what's next" to what preceded it. In that sense, every period following another is post-*something*. The question for us is: What has preceded us that is now dismantling, mutating, or disappearing?

Modernity is the culmination of the Enlightenment, a historical-philosophical development that began well before the Protestant Reformation and has extended to its logical conclusion in our own scientific age. There has been no sudden break, any more than the Renaissance ended the medieval period instantly, but it has moved forward in a slow, deliberate process. The presuppositions of modernity are many, but for our worship life, its most salient ones are two:

- Rationality is the measure of all truth, and reason is the chief means to knowledge. Nonrational knowing is always subservient to rational knowing, or else it is discounted entirely. Things we can't prove or understand don't really exist. If we can't measure, analyze, or quantify it, it isn't real, or we can't say anything meaningful about it. Logic is more important than the senses, which should be mistrusted. Body—as opposed to mind—is something to be subdued, not claimed.

- Certain unrivaled universal principles, structural absolutes, and singular norms are present in all cultures, everywhere, through all time. These are deduced through reason and can be proved through rational argument. Because reason is its own revelation, these universals are apparent in truth, beauty, morals, politics, human rights, family life, and religious life.

First, let it be said that the Enlightenment was not all bad; we would all be the poorer without it. Who would want to continue living with a medieval worldview, a life determined by superstition, magic, and unchallenged authorities? Not I and probably not most.

My own religious tradition is the Disciples of Christ, and our founders were people of their time, strongly influenced by such rationalists as John Locke. This philosophy and worldview informs not only church life—in a very democratic way—but also scriptural interpretation and worship styles. Alexander Campbell, our preeminent theologian and apologist in the first generation of our movement, claimed that the gospel was perfectly reasonable. According to Campbell, one needed only to approach it rationally, and its truth would spring forth apparent.

On the one hand, I am pleased that the Campbell side of our tradition includes rational categories of analysis for approaching sacred texts. However, I am also quite certain that the philosophical modernity of Campbell's thesis is not entirely adequate for this reason: The gospel is *not* entirely reasonable, nor can it be approached as so. It is replete with the most unreasonable call to existence one could ever imagine. Moreover, postmodern persons know this, even if they are unable to articulate it.

The point is *not* that Enlightenment thought is bad, or entirely irrelevant, or should be discarded. The point *is* that its presuppositions are left wanting for balance. Modernity now needs to be balanced by its omissions, and there is no place in the body of Christ where this is needed more than in worship.

Postmodern culture now questions modernity's excessive rationalism. In current culture, we often find the tension between these worlds best portrayed in television and movies. Who can miss it in the oppositional yet complementary duo of agents Mulder and Scully in the *X Files*? or Captain Kirk and Mr. Spock in *Star Trek*? or Bayliss and Pembleton in *Homicide*? Intuitive believer and scientific modernist unite as partners. There is tension there and conflict, but also the seeking of completeness on the part of each. The missing aspects are found in the other.

Postmodern culture also knows that the underpinnings of truth and beauty are relative, not absolute. As a cursory summary of the history of art, music, literature, architecture, psychological schools, fashion, social theories and scientific dogma shows, those who have the power both write the history and determine what is universal. Claims about absolute structures remain suspect.

A postmodern understands how the context of culture often shapes its meanings. One culture cannot use an external ruler to measure the internal validity of another culture's symbols and way of being. In the same way that a non-Christian can never fully understand what it means to take bread and wine in communion with Christ, so a non-Muslim can never fully comprehend what it means to make the hajj to Mecca. Although both groups may understand in general the importance of, say, sacred meals and pilgrimages, only insiders can fully know the import of their own tradition's symbolic meanings. These kinds of things cannot be fairly understood or critiqued from the outside.

The community itself, therefore, defines its own essentials, rituals, convictions, and peculiar way of life. It may not make sense according to external measurements, as part of the cacophony of cultural noise, but that is unimportant. Its validity does not derive from a supposedly objective assessment from the outside. Instead, the community of faith finds its own story and song. When it sings in tune and with conviction, it will carry on a meaningful apologetic with the world while not worrying too much about what the world might think of it.

Each religious tradition and culture has its language. This language is expressed in its common life and understandings, but it is most explicit in the liturgy. Coming to believe is similar to learning a language. This has to do not only with vocabulary and syntax but also with the worldview and sacred meanings held by it. Doxology, eucharist, confession, and prayer all have their place and function within the language. Conversion to this special religious language requires a Berlitz course in the Christian tradition. Over time, one accumulates an increasing knowledge of what is embedded in that acquired tongue.

Worshiping communities are relevant *not* to the degree that they ask what is pleasing, attractive, or palatable to the prevailing culture. They *are* relevant if they become expert in speaking and teaching their language in different contexts and to persons who may know fewer verbs and nouns than their neighbor. This is what makes them relevant. As language and thought are integrally connected, so liturgy lives by the transcendent power of God that fills its speaking.

For the church of the postmodern time this includes the reintroduction of nonrational categories of knowing—the ineffable, mysterious, and awe-inspiring—back into our worship. It is a reintroduction because it existed in many of the world's liturgies before they were reasoned away. When the Reformed tradition painted over the art in its churches, it made understandable theological statements for its time. It was compelled to make corrections to perceived idolatry while exalting the place of the Word. What was lost under the paint, however, was the visual, sensual, aesthetic, and iconic pathway through which rationality could never pass by itself. Postmoderns want to scrub down these concealed artifacts with industrial-strength paint remover in order to reexpose them.

The church of a postmodern culture knows that meanings are *assigned* to the world—by individual persons, traditions, revelations—but that these meanings are not always automatically present or apparent, especially across cultures. Postmodernity holds some suspicion toward claims of objectivity because those decisions are made by those who hold enough power to make them to their advantage. Feminist movements have taught us this with clarity. Truth is received and mediated in concrete contexts and cultures. In the same way, notions of what is and is not "good" worship are also assigned by particular communities and individual persons who have the power to do so.

Postmoderns also live in the time of the new great revolution in communication. Whole universities, cities, and homes are hardwired to the cyberworld. Entire generations of GenXers and Millennials take it for granted that the electronic revolution is a given of modern life.

Cultures have evolved along multiple communication pathways. Sometimes these pathways overlap and function simultaneously. In other instances, one replaces another. The process has moved from oral tradition to papyrus scrolls to codices; from Guttenberg's printing press to telegraphs to phones; from radio to television to videotape; from e-mail to the Internet to fully digital culture. The church will have to discern what part and place this communication revolution will play in our religious and liturgical life. Regardless of the choices that are made, it will be at the church's peril that we ignore this reality of everyday life.

Whether we incorporate digital communication in our worship or instead use worship as a radical, countercultural *fast* from the attacking stream of data, a mindful decision must be made and made in particular contexts. Whether the call to worship of the future contains, "This is the day the Lord has made… please put on your virtual reality visors," or "This is the day the Lord has made…please turn off your cell phones, beepers, and Palm Pilots—be still and know that God is God!" the church must decide.

As digitally meditated communication has created a new *image-laden culture* operating alongside a continuing *print culture*, a fascinating connection between premodernity and postmodernity has bubbled to the surface. In the same way that present virtual forms of reality rely on electronically generated images and signs, so premodern culture depended on everything from catacomb art to elaborate stained-glass representations to the sacred dramatic troupes of the Middle Ages. There is a connection, and it is a powerful one, but these ways of apprehending reality are at the same time similar and distinct.

The differences between these two times of history are marked. By comparison with the earlier, more structured, comprehensive, and mythically integrated notions of reality, our own electronic age is disjointed and chaotic. The postmodern understanding of sacred story also differs from its predecessor's. It holds the self-conscious awareness that story is just that—a means to convey truth; a parable is known to be a parable, a myth to be a myth, and an apocalyptic scenario the extension of intense hopes. This is different from a premodern naïveté, taking the text at face value without knowing what is speaking and how. Postmoderns may be captured by myths, but they know how they are being captured.

The worldviews of premodernity and postmodernity differ, but the *way* in which reality is mediated—whether by iconography or Web site flash technology—is similar. Dependency on visual, sensory, experiential, and embodied sign joins them together in interesting ways. Therefore, the postmodern connection with the ancient can be naturally strong. This means that ancient symbol, ritual, processions, sensory aids, smells, bells, and candles all bridge easily into postmodern consciousness.

The person who listens easily to Jay Leno on *The Tonight Show* and understands the *way* in which his show is now produced, in contrast to when Johnny Carson hosted the show, may more easily visualize and connect with the fantastic images found in the book of Revelation. He or she may be more satisfied with simply *experiencing* them without a comprehensive rational explanation. Those who enjoy the chaos comedy of the absurd, such as *Seinfeld* or *Saturday Night Live,* as opposed to the humor of the Bob Hope generation, will intuitively identify with slice-of-life biblical episodes that do not always have tidy and systematic beginnings and endings. Loose ends are expected as part of the randomness and complexity of life.

They will *not* do so well with long, sustained, and careful arguments, and this may be the primary challenge of both teaching and preaching today. If our now legendary "pulpit princes" of yesteryear were to visit us today, and not change either their rhetoric or content, they would meet with little success. The hour or two-hour long "list" sermons of one hundred fifty years ago, full of doctrinal definitions and clarifications, would be preached to empty churches. The "three points and a poem" sermons of the early twentieth century would (and do) suffer the same fate. Of course, the good apologists of every age have adapted to their contexts, and we would expect that they would adapt if they were with us!

For Christian worship, this provides a daunting challenge: Worldviews overlap. Hegemony in worship style no longer exists. No single kind of music has a corner on mediating religious truth. The ways that religious experience and our reflection on it take place in the gathered community are both the same and different. Then again, this is exactly what Christians have faced throughout the centuries. It has been the source of both building traditions and reforming them. These transitions have never been easy, neat, or clean. Just as today, our brothers and sisters often found themselves perplexed and uncertain about what their future would hold.

As postmodern worship reclaims lost nonrational and mysterious dimensions, some notions of control have to be released. In the same way that a joke is ruined if you have to explain the punch line, so the power of symbol carries its own impact and is often undermined by undue explanation. This may be uncomfortable for modernists who want to define every aspect and coordinate, but this freedom is exactly what powerful symbols require.

Here is the challenge for a church that is surrounded, as was Justin Martyr, by both nonbelieving and multiple-faith cultures: How to be apologists and share the faith, but allow sacred story and symbol to speak for themselves.

This should include reasonable access to liturgical meanings. For instance, periodic teaching on the meaning of, say, baptism or the Lord's supper is essential. In the moment of celebration, however, we must allow seekers and practicing Christians alike to be confronted by the *transcendent beyond* in their midst. In this way a clear Christian voice may be not only heard and understood but also experienced in deep, ineffable places.

This requires margins of intellectual and emotional space in which a worshiper may swim. Intentional silence is the locale of much of this, but so is meditative chant or simple song. It is no wonder that Taizé services or the singing of scriptural choruses have taken on such popularity in recent years. Functioning alongside poetic hymn forms with several verses, simple mantralike repetition may internalize deep truths.

The way we use words is changing as well. Before the modern era, it was not considered unusual at all for scripture to be interpreted allegorically or metaphorically. The idea that there is one fixed meaning for each text is a modern anomaly, certainly foreign to the writers of what we now have as sacred scripture. In the rabbinic tradition, each word of Torah was understood to resemble a diamond—to have a thousand facets. With the rise of scientific rationalism, this mystery of ever-speaking, never-exhausted source of wisdom and revelation was lost.

The historical-critical method, for instance, has been of unparalleled value when it comes to analyzing the world behind the text or the redactic distinctions between authors. As such, it held and holds great importance for understanding and interpretation. Such tools, however, are clearly children of the Enlightenment, and their rationalistic method also obscures certain kinds of knowing. The nature of freely working scripture in transforming worship is its ability to move to the places where spiritual apprehension is; each person is allowed to hear it in her or his own place on many different levels. This is one of the valuable contributions of narrative theology and the method of a narrative biblical hermeneutic.

Worship in the era of modernity primarily depended on an extensive canon of written text, often in print form in the hands of worshipers and on the podiums of preachers. This mediating function of the printed text fostered a kind of relationship of distance between worshiper and worship leaders and, ultimately, between the worshiper and the Holy. The evidence of misunderstanding the differences between print-based and image-based communication is often found in well-meaning persons who hastily erect their projection screens in worship spaces but do not carefully consider what they will do with them. A projected sermon outline with PowerPoint® bullets is nothing more than boardroom modernity in electronic form. The fact that it is projected digitally is beside the point; that is just the delivery system. *It remains patently print culture.*

With the advent of the postprint digital revolution, a whole new way of learning and knowing is taking place. There is now emerging a powerful new shaping of oral-narrative communication. Visual-symbolic images now mediate truths and meaning in ways that are accessible to contemporary culture. In this milieu, heavy print-culture worship with its wall of words is destined to lead people away from a deep and meaningful encounter with God.

The implications for preaching in particular are numerous. Good communication today makes contact quickly, casts evocative images, and presents a compelling narrative of both the text and of life.

In a worship setting, powerful reading of scripture may be dramatized without explanation or preached not so much as information to be passed but as mystery to behold. Is there a place for teaching and didactic explanation? Of course, but will we also allow the texts a freedom to speak for themselves? All of us have witnessed the distorted use of scripture too much not to be concerned. In light of the egregious uses of scripture, the reading of bias and even hatred into texts, can that be risked? Or is it not a question of either-or? Is it rather a delicate dance of analysis and mystery, correctives along the way, in which worshipers ask questions of sacred texts and *the texts ask questions of them*?

Many congregations study the lectionary texts used in worship in small groups or classes. They engage the texts in community, often discussing backgrounds, sources, tensions, and implications for common or individual life. This can partner with what is experienced in the sacred worship locale, where the light falls on the page in a different way. After reflection on a text, windows open wider with its telling, to be sure. However, do we have the courage to set the text free to roam the room and capture whom it will?

In our congregation, we recently hosted a guest biblical storyteller. That's what he did; he enacted, told, and shared biblical stories. He did not provide explanation as he went; he told the stories. Young teenagers were present, those meisters of digital culture and captains of virtual reality, and they sat on the edges of their seats, mouths open wide as they listened to the *telling* of the sacred stories. A strange new world for them? Remote, far-off, and perplexing? Most surely. Perhaps this is exactly why they were intrigued and wanted more.

For the enthusiasts of the Corinthian church, the apostle Paul counseled interpretation of their ecstatic experience (1 Cor. 14). After all, how else could a visitor understand this strange, new world? A thoughtful faith reflects on its own experience. A caring faith helps the hungry to get to the bread. Rational and nonrational categories of experience need one another. We must strike the balance as well.

Consider the early worship clues left behind for us by our Christian predecessors in the earliest generation. Postmodernity may learn from premodernity if it will. They had an order of worship, but no printed worship bulletin. Sacred texts were read or sung. Edifying commentary was made on the texts. Prayers were uttered that were often prescribed, but they were memorized not read. There was recitation and singing of psalms. The sacred meal was shared, and then they went forth with blessing. They shared a tradition known by heart and communicated by oral practice.

In many respects, our postmodern worship journey is similar to the movie title *Back to the Future,* but only in some respects. Certainly, this is *not* a theological journey back behind the Enlightenment. It *is,* however, a journey to a place where the theological world is built by the power of symbol, narrative, color, art, sign, icon, multisensory experience, and community rituals.

Just recently I was worshiping in one of our services and the acolyte of the day was sitting beside me. During the service of the table, as the other pastor lifted the communion elements and intoned the words of institution, "This is my body, broken for you...," our young acolyte whispered every word right along with him. He was not reading the words off a printed bulletin. They were words emblazoned on his heart, and he recited them wide-eyed as the bread was being torn in two. It doesn't get better than this.

This is a journey to a place where the community of faith speaks with its own voice, dances on its own tradition, and dares to teach it to those who would enter its domain. This is a journey to where truth is apprehended and revealed in both rational and experiential nonrational ways. This is a journey into apologetics in which an ongoing conversation is generated with the culture and context in which the church is found. This is a journey to a place where the future is taken as seriously as the past and the resurrection of hope is expected in every worship experience. By this the gospel of Jesus Christ continues—in its radical freedom—to transform individual persons and communities and the world in which they live.

CHAPTER FOUR

One Song, Many Voices

Context, Tradition, and Culture

*And the four living creatures, each of them with six wings,
are full of eyes all around and inside. Day and night
without ceasing they sing,*

> *"Holy, holy, holy,*
> *the Lord God the Almighty,*
> *who was and is and is to come."*

REVELATION 4:8

In a conversation with an African American pastor serving in the inner city, I learned what "alternative worship" meant for him in his context. It was not what white Christians might expect—a high-energy, praise-testifying service out of the black tradition. That, said he, was "traditional" for him. Rather, in a social setting of gangs, violence, and noise, the sanctuary was opened in the evening. People were invited to enter in silence, lay on their backs in the aisles and on the pews, and stare at the ceiling of the sanctuary as Renaissance motets and Baroque fugues enfolded them in a newly created world.

In the jazz-infected corners of St. Louis, a city that laps up jazz as if it were cream, another church opens its doors to the city and offers a Sunday evening blues service. It's simple, soulful, and moving. Afterward they move downstairs to the fellowship hall where they share a communion of bread and soup around the tables.

What do these two congregations have in common? They took their cultural contexts seriously and attempted to offer faithful worship that touches the soul.

As the Christian language holds its core conviction, hope, unity, and mission as part of its theological syntax and grammar, its varying styles of worship are like *dialects* within the same native tongue. The same language is modified in colloquial and stylized ways according to its context. It may contain phrases and newly coined words that have arisen from peculiar histories.

Whatever dialect carries the liturgy, however the accents are spoken, it must be the language of the *grand story,* recognizable as the language of the Christian story. All services of worship, regardless of cultural styles, need to be grounded in certain origins and draw on certain powers. From what does this ritual life spring? From the life-giving, world-creating, life-transforming good news of Jesus Christ? Or does it originate with something else? If the lifeblood of worship only runs toward the adoration of popular culture, where does that take people? Is the cultural form the *servant* of the grand story or does it come to be worshiped for its own sake?

With the world window open, Christians now look out on a menagerie of Christian cultures and their worships. What they find is often inspiring and more than a little perplexing.

It does not surprise us that the most rapidly growing Christian movements in the world—in Africa, Latin America, Asia—have exuberant, mysterious, healing, storytelling communities of faith. As middle American Protestants open their liturgical windows and take a deep breath, the air of the multicultural church is full of oxygen. In its inhaling, worlds have been enlarged, possibilities increased, and prayerful ecumenical life strengthened.

Missionaries who return from assignments in other cultures bring their own experience of and connection with multicultural worship. The liturgical sharing of the World Council of Churches has left a legacy of ecumenical world Christian music unequaled in its breadth. Worship life at the Ecumenical Institute at Bossey, Switzerland, or at the General Assemblies of the World Council has shaped thousands of Christians in the richness of a world worship culture. Other examples are the worship and music of Taizé and the Iona community and how they have made their way into the standard repertoire of many hymnals.

This does not mean, however, that people of integrity unthinkingly adopt the religious forms and styles of those sisters and brothers. Such borrowing is not to be taken lightly. Simple appropriation denies the uniqueness of another culture's particularity. *Grateful borrowing* of another tradition, on the other hand, may strengthen and enrich. With due tribute and recognition, this worship not only adds to the texture of our own but also creates an atmosphere of unity. Finally, the challenge is to determine just *how* a transforming multicultural worship can be shared, celebrated, and known in one's own context.

In recent mission trips to Ecuador, our mission teams have experienced indigenous worship forms of the Indian communities and also the newly syncretized forms of mestizo youth culture. As in most continents that hold the influences of their original traditions and also those of the colonial period, worship in Latin America is a combination of ancient custom and the legacy of the Northern or Western worship. It is the source of no little challenge for present-day Christians to reclaim their own precolonial culture while holding on to the Christian proclamation. The answer to the question is now being given in several ways.

The most recent adaptations in urban centers have been with the popular worship and music culture of the North. Because popular youth culture worship is broadcast on television and recording artists—both Northern and local—make the stadium rounds, these influences have made their way into worship.

The first wave of worship revisionism in Ecuador directly reshaped mestizo worship in smaller and larger cities in the 1990s. The later wave, which first hit Ecuador in 2001, struck the shores of the indigenous Indian youth, young people who don Palm Pilots under ponchos and send e-mails to friends from coffee shops beside open air markets. These young people took the new worship to large regional gatherings of the indigenous churches. For the first time, the native drums, flutes, and acoustic guitars were joined by electronic keyboards, drum sets, and microphones. Most importantly, the worship style of neoevangelicalism elbowed its way onto the stage without apology. Elders sat stunned and bemused. This new wave has not made its way back to the small villages and towns in which they live, however. Like most of those in middle North America, rural areas hold more tenaciously to tradition.

The verdict is not yet in on whether these influences will last or what overall impact they will have. Younger Christians are not particularly worried about those questions, but older, longer-term Christians are. They wonder how this works with their established traditions or if the traditions will be lost. They worry that their youth will be overtaken by a new colonialism of a foreign culture. They are concerned that this reaches far beyond style into theology itself.

These Ecuadorian elders struggle with the same questions that are pondered by the leaders of most typical congregations in Anytown, USA. The world church is already here, and the globalization of worship has already arrived. How shall one relate to it, appropriate it, critique it, or enter into it?

Most innovating worship emerges as an attempt to bridge a gap between church and culture as Christians reach out as apologists. As we have seen, this is not new. It is part and parcel of the mission of the church and the evolution of the liturgy through the centuries. Static forms go the way of museums, but through a dynamic process of expanding and contracting, forming and reforming, creating and recreating, a new song continues to appear.

Faithful creating of new worship forms requires interplay between tradition and experience, form and freedom, and theology and culture. Like the best jazz music, a balance is found between the chordal and melodic structure of the tune on the one hand, and free improvisation on the other. Good liturgical improvisation shows itself most clearly as it reaches into three current slices of context: generation, situation, and culture.

These contexts combine in an amalgam of influence, shaping the ways of perceiving the world and reflecting the peculiar challenges faced by a particular generation. Ways of worship are shaped by these differences.

In terms of *generation,* world events shape the consciousness of young people for years to come. The World War II generation, for instance, has very different feelings about structure and delaying gratification for the common good than, say, their Baby Boomer children. Their understanding of the world is different, and therefore their understanding of God moving in the world and their worship of God are different as well.

The life *situation* of technology-equipped fifteen-year-olds living in a blended family following September 11 is quite different from that of their grandparents, who have memories of Cold War civil-defense drills and the specter of nuclear war. The way in which not only information but also *reality* is mediated differs greatly from those preceding them by only a slim ten years.

More than that, one's inherited and created *culture* provides music, art, literature, politics, folkways, and dominant social values—a little symbolic world to understand the world. For example, the Baby Boomers who were shaped by a dominant therapeutic culture often persist in speaking in recovery and psychological terms to generations that both precede and follow them. When no contact is achieved, they withdraw, perplexed and confused. Wouldn't everyone understand the world this way?

The dialects of worship must be spoken while knowing that these slices of context are always at work—generation, situation, and culture.

Certainly, multiple dialects of worship language may be spoken in the same congregation. It is not uncommon for churches to offer two or more worship experiences, all of which speak in a slightly different accent. In addition, as people from the outside visit the symbolic Christian world, they gain access to it through a multidialect smorgasbord of opportunities under one congregational umbrella.

What about a *metaworship* language, a liturgical vernacular that might act as *Java*, the computer language that talks to all other computer languages? How can the power of the gospel find its transcultural voice in us? Can the Ancient of Days be worshiped with a new song, and where?

In postmodern life, the sign markers are several, and they often reach across many contexts. In *metaworship,* we may take tradition and context seriously and bridge

- experience with explanation
- sense with thought
- image with words
- creativity with form
- silence with sound
- confession with praise

Metaworship, at its best, will create sacred space and liturgy where the Holy is *experienced* and felt as well as cognitively known; spiritual passion is expressed; thoughtfulness sharpened; and all the senses are engaged. Sound, image, light, taste, touch, and smell compose a sacramental celebration of God incarnated in the whole good and created order, an outward reflection of transcendent graces.

Metaworship, at its best, will reclaim the full *participation* of the whole people of God. Does our worship foster passivity or active enactment in the gathered community? Is the focus on glorifying the God of heaven and earth in a community of belonging and in which all serve as priests to the other? Are Christians encouraged to draw the best of their thinking and art into the creation of liturgy and also engage in its leadership?

Metaworship, at its best, will be like a scribe of the kingdom who draws out of the treasure chest *that which is old and new.* Religious communities live in the currents of traditions, combinations of beliefs, practices, and norms that shape the very identity of a people. Vital worshiping communities will re-present tradition in a new light, telling its story and encouraging ongoing conversation with it.

Metaworship, at its best, will reclaim the *use of powerful images* that were lost to print-culture liturgy. Its appearance will more resemble an illuminated manuscript than the page of a dictionary. Images lie close to the center of human consciousness, and in particular religious experience. Transforming communities of faith will find graphic ways to wrap the people around their symbols, whether in physical or virtual space. The reclaiming of preprint oral culture will provide a bridge to postmodern culture.

Metaworship, at its best, will take the *context of the culture* seriously and engage with it. This includes not only the tools by which the message must be communicated but also the existential need in the culture. Loneliness, broad mobility of families, social unrest, oppression, war, unemployment, and addiction—they all make up the mission field of the church and the place where worship engages with the people. The cultural context also includes its own lively artistic traditions, ways of viewing the world and shaping its social life.

Metaworship, at its best, will reclaim the place of *communal rituals.* They will become more, not less important in the future. Rites of passage for infants, children, youth, and adults; enactment of powerful truths in times of crisis; and common prayer in the particular junctures of collective or personal life will be symbolized in the midst of the community's drama of faith. This will include storytelling, dance, meals, song, play, and prayer.

Metaworship, at its best, will embody what transforming worship always has. It will connect the gathered pilgrims to the Great Mystery and to one another, sweeping them toward a future of hope.

CHAPTER FIVE

Illusions of Originality

Re-creating with What Already Is

All streams run to the sea,
    but the sea is not full;
to the place where the streams flow,
    there they continue to flow...
What has been is what will be,
    and what has been done is what will be done;
    there is nothing new under the sun.

ECCLESIASTES 1:7, 9

One path of worship invigoration today is to offer varied kinds of worship alternatives. As we have seen, the reformation of the liturgy is not a new project, one unique to our time. It is the continuation of a tradition that is continually modified. These changes in worship styles may reflect actual theological and philosophical shifts or merely the adaptation of cultural externals. If the culture is taken seriously, worship form may adapt in order to become a new vehicle to carry an eternal cargo; worship may deliver its essentials to new generations in new contexts, but not automatically so. To make only external and stylistic changes in the *vehicle* is not necessarily to be the church reformed, always reforming. The *cargo itself* is the thing, and no amount of tinkering under the hood will propel a car without an engine. At least not for long.

In a false rush toward relevance, or in an attempt to bolster sagging membership rolls, congregations and their leaders often plunge unthinkingly into the torrents of unknown worship streams. The worst-case scenarios are often just that, the worst: the absence of serious reflection among leaders, the exclusion of the congregation in decision making, the importing of elements foreign to one's own tradition, and escalating conflict. This lack of planning and its corresponding rush to do something, *anything* different often become a shooting star on the worship horizon. "Remember when they experimented with something different down in the fellowship hall? Was that last summer, or the summer before? Hope they got *that* out of their system."

On the other hand, faithful congregations have opened themselves to new ways of worship that have brought about real and enduring transformation. These reforms have not necessarily been associated with the churchly trends of the moment. Many congregations have accomplished this by simply accenting what they do best, reclaiming lost traditions, or involving a greater participation of the membership in its worship planning and leadership.

For many other congregations the creation of new and transforming worship has required a sojourn outside the conventional—at least the conventional as known within their tradition. Dynamic congregations have not simply appropriated the styles and content of the growing independent church in the metal building on the edge of town. They have been more thoughtful than that, and it shows.

Although there are many alternative variations of worship form in our time, a few are singled out time and again as *the* stereotypical models. These darlings of the worship horizon often serve as the case *du jour*, whether one is presenting them in a favorable or unfavorable light. On the one hand, they are cited as evidence for just how *bad* it can get: "Just entertainment; all emotion, no depth; focus not on God, but on the needs of the consumer-worshiper." Or in an enthusiastic *endorsement* of the success they are having on the other side of the street: "Go high tech; every message a PowerPoint® message; rent the band now." Both arguments share the same deficit. They miss the simple fact that congregations are innovating *many* different forms of worship, and what one identifies as a beginning point or norm will determine, to a great extent, the kind of outcome that will be realized. Consider just a few of the predominant innovating or alternative worship models:

Liturgical Stream: Plugs current content and artistic idioms into the traditional forms of a fairly high-print historic liturgy. Many examples are found in the Roman Catholic and Lutheran traditions. The primary distinctions between more conventional and alternative liturgical services might be in levels of formality and types of musical choices and leadership. In many cases, the same prayer book is used for both.

Seeker–Presentational Stream: Offers a largely non-participatory, highly polished package of popular music, drama, media, and motivational messages in a theaterlike setting. It attempts to reach popular culture where it lives on its own terms. There is an avoidance of so-called liturgical impediments that might confuse seekers and leave them feeling lost. Accent is on access, getting new people there and discipling them later.

Praise–Message Stream: Moves the worshipers with a highly participatory, extended period of frequently repeating choruses and easily singable hymns. This is followed by a lengthy teaching-style message that instructs worshipers by an exposition of biblical texts that are applied to Christian living.

Worshipers are sometimes encouraged to "fill in the blanks" of the teaching session on provided bulletins. Worshipers are expected to participate by doing rather than by observing.

Historic-Ecumenical Stream: Makes use of the historic-ecumenical form of the liturgy while adopting a non–print-culture service that is highly participatory. It relies heavily on symbols and rituals; maintains theological integrity, however the form is modified; and extends a global outlook through its music, prayers, and teaching. Messages often hold a combination of inspirational and teaching elements meant to speak to seasoned and new Christians alike.

A simple survey of this worship landscape uncovers some remarkable contrasts—contrasts that require thoughtful choices:

- Is the service going to be delivered primarily in print-driven terms or nonprint, oral tradition? or a combination thereof? How will images be employed? with physical representations? digital projection? by the use of language and storytelling?
- What is the role of the congregation? Participatory or observatory? Is the music presented *to* the congregation or shared *by* the congregation? Is prayer corporate, and if so, how? Is the Lord's Prayer recited or sung? Is there any congregational movement in the service? If dramatic arts are employed, how are they used? in skits, the enactment of scripture, sermon monologues? Are prayers read collectively or offered by one on behalf of all? How does laity provide actual leadership in services? and children and youth?
- Are sacraments, rituals, symbols, and ceremony avoided or accentuated? Is the Lord's table a centerpiece around which the service orients? Do baptisms demand special emphasis, teaching, and celebration of the whole community, or are they frequently held in private? Is color and sacred decor used to signify a change of season or theme? Are guiding symbols employed to redirect

consciousness, or does worship occur in a minimalist, nonadorned space? Are vestments avoided or creatively employed?

- How is scripture used? as a supplement or as proof-texting for the message? Is it read or enacted as part of the tradition that has a life of its own and may speak for itself? Is there a thematic tie to liturgical seasons of the year and traditional lections, or is scripture only heard in conjunction with the sermon?
- Is the primary goal of the message to teach the faith to new Christians or to represent the Christian story for persons at many places of faith formation? Is the preaching moment seen as an opportunity to pass on information, foster conversion, form Christian souls, or motivate the community to faithfulness? Is proclamation most occupied with explanation or with a parabolic disruption of what is already believed?
- Is the action of worship taking place primarily among a small group of leaders in the chancel area or within the gathered community itself? Is there a sense of transcendence, otherness, sacredness—even when the focus is on the spirit moving among flesh and blood people?
- What sort of underlying shape or structure of worship is employed? Is it based on ecumenical or historic patterns of the liturgy? revivalist camp meetings? theater productions? talk shows? MTV-style rapid fire, loosely connected, and sometimes-contradictory fragments? Is the focus on subjective experience or objective truth? Is it world-related and ecumenically shaped? or radically personalized and localized?
- Is communication digitally mediated and technologically driven? How much dependence is there on technology?

Is there really nothing new under the sun? Certainly all the raw matter is already here, but the living, creating, ever-changing God continues to create and cocreate with us. The

Spirit continues to blow through the church, inspiring us to put the old matter together in new and creative ways, in this particular time and place, shaped as we are by our tradition, theology, context, and culture. When we say we want to innovate new worship forms in our communities, what do we mean? to what end? and with what starting places?

In our present culture, two powerful worship impulses are moving parallel to each other. There is a longing to return to or to find grounded, ancient traditions and a simultaneous search for spiritual life in culturally relevant terms. Both movements have strength, often determined by their cultural locations. Both searches are taking place in our speed of light, technological, multicultural, and postmodern culture. Both tracks look for an anchor in the absence of structural absolutes. Both ask where the holy is to be found, and in ways that speak immediately with a compelling voice. In either quest, the questions are similar: How can I find a sense of the sacred and meaning for living when I want more than anything else to believe, hope, and love? Where is the rootedness beyond myself? How can it make a real difference?

The movement toward historic worship often finds roots, tradition, mystery, continuity, structure, rituals of passage, and a distinctive theological narrative. Worship models that resonate with popular culture frequently offer freedom, spontaneity, exuberance, personal community, and familiar technological and musical idioms. These characteristics are not mutually exclusive, of course, but certain accents are found in one more than the other.

The way faithful people answer these questions shapes not only the worship of a congregation but also the congregation itself.

Of course, there is the temptation to create new congregational patterns for the wrong reasons. If new worship moves are made not because they are richer, fuller, and deeper, but because they require less work and are easier to manage, a weaker worship is assured. If the ingredients of several services are stirred haphazardly together in the interest of "compromise," the end product is most often a strange-tasting stew of the lowest common denominator. If an unconscious striving for uniformity prevails, even though it *poses* as a quest for unity, unique flavors within a congregation will be lost.

How can a congregation bring together a convergence of the rooted, God-centered, sacramental, transcendent, historic liturgy that also makes meaningful contact with the postmodern culture?

The way to transforming worship requires sustained preparation, prayer, reading, discernment, study, and visitation of other congregations. The unity of the body requires a process in which the leadership and membership of the congregation continue to be involved. Only in this way can the vision and future of the church dance with its tradition.

CHAPTER SIX

Out of the Treasure Chest

Something New and Something Old

"Every scribe who has been trained for the kingdom of heaven is like the master of the household who brings out of his treasure what is new and what is old."

MATTHEW 13:52

Our exploration of the early synagogue service and table fellowship of the Jesus movement has led us to the doorstep of the nascent beginnings of Christian worship. Over time and in different contexts, the ancient patterns evolved and expanded with increasing complexity and ornamentation. One of the frequent results of reform in the church was reform in the liturgy, and in those times of reform, the content of the liturgy frequently changed and simplified. This cyclic and reforming process of expansion and contraction continued into the twentieth century and has continued to move on many different levels.

As a product of the ecumenical movement of the twentieth century, a consensus grew surrounding the shape of the ancient liturgy. With the beginning identification of the larger twofold pattern of *Word and table*, the consensus grew to include a fourfold pattern of *gathering, Word, table, and dismissal*. Depending on the tradition of the local worshiping community, this fourfold pattern can be adopted as the basic structure over which remarkable liturgical freedom may take place.

Simultaneous with this consensus toward the fourfold liturgical pattern we have become aware of the distinctive and powerful influences of postmodern thought and perception.

Some who embraced the insights of postmodern thought concluded that the historic forms only represented a hindrance in accomplishing their ends. For these persons, reformation would not be limited to contraction, reduction, and simplification. In their haste, they also discarded the underlying historic and ecumenical pattern of Christian worship of the ages. Not only was this move unnecessary but it also cut the church's anchor line. No matter what was happening on deck, the ship itself was afloat.

This false assumption misses a simple but profound connection, namely, that this postmodern era is in many ways like the first three centuries in which Christianity emerged. Although theologically and philosophically distinct, the contexts of both pre-Christian and post-Christian culture hold crucial elements in common, not the least of which are secularism, religious pluralism, and deep spiritual hunger. These two eras also parallel each other in ways by which reality is mediated and the type of engagement that is required to reach their cultures. This present postmodern situation calls forth the best from both our tradition *and* our creativity. It requires bold and honest articulation of the grand narrative that is ours.

If we were to stand atop the historic-ecumenical pattern of worship while simultaneously taking the currents of postmodern culture seriously, what kind of worship would emerge? Neither the caretaker function of traditionalism nor the raw pragmatism of consumer culture will do. However, the confluence of this ancient core with postmodern thought provides a genuine opportunity for transforming worship to emerge among the people of God—*metaworship standing atop firm foundations.*

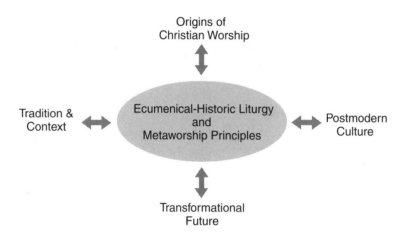

Origins of
Christian Worship

Tradition &
Context

Ecumenical-Historic Liturgy
and
Metaworship Principles

Postmodern
Culture

Transformational
Future

The use of the historic fourfold pattern may be in elaborate or minimalist forms. In terms of structure, it may act as the foundation for liturgical moves on top of or within it. In some of the newer, post–print-culture, alternative worship communities, this form is represented not by a printed order at all, but by a worship "grid" held only by worship planners and leaders. The grid contains "moves" that are defined by multisensory experience. For instance, one could construct a worship grid using the fourfold pattern and accompanying media shown on page 55 for the guiding theme of "building on the rock."

Such minimalist patterns of Christian celebration seem extreme, and yet throughout the world, such expressions are not rare. A worship grid such as this does not contain all the theology or content of such a worship experience, but it does demonstrate the possibilities of combining the fourfold pattern with metaworship principles. The same kind of thing might be accomplished in a more customary worship format and space, embodying creative use of the fourfold pattern and historic-liturgical content:

Gathering
Act of Praise
Psalms, Hymns, Gloria

Word
Scripture Lessons
Message
Historic Confession of Faith

Table
Prayer
Lord's Prayer
Passing the Peace
Offering of the People
The Eucharist

Dismissal
Benediction
Song of Sending

Again, though the degree of elaboration depends on the particular tradition and community, the form remains basically the same.

Structure, however, is not the only thing that defines the ecumenical-historic liturgy. Identifiable, repeating, and remembered rituals and words serve to reinforce and strengthen the worship experience. This is the power of knowing one's tradition by heart and knowing it with others.

PATTERN	WORDS	ACTIONS	MUSIC	IMAGES
GATHERING	Poem: "Bricks, Rising and Falling"	Setting of table by people wearing construction belts and overalls	Instrumental loop	Projected icon of pile of bricks
WORD	Telling of Matthew 11; meditation	Two people stacking bricks	Recorded sounds of hammering and construction	Videotape of bricklayers building a wall
TABLE	Intercessory prayer offered as communion loaf is passed among worshipers, who come forward for communion by intinction	Communicants light candles around altar area on the way to communing	Chant: "Jesus, Remember Me"	Loaf and cup sitting on top of several bricks
DISMISSAL	Call and response: Sending forth with words of the Great Commission	Worshipers are given prayers rolled as scrolls— containing a prayer based on Matthew 11	Song: "Go Out with Joy"	Image of carpenter walking out of door into world

When a congregation hears the call to prayer, "The Lord be with you," and knows from memory to respond, "and with your spirit," they ready themselves for prayer in unconscious ways. The repeating ritual has done this for them. In the same way that the house lights dim before the symphony's first note breaks the silence, ritual signs prepare the individual person and the community to dip into their repertoire of remembered and treasured spiritual pathways. Even the worshiping communities that go to great lengths to eschew all liturgical frameworks have their unwritten codes, rituals, and languages that provide cues to the community—almost always in the same ways—that something is about to happen.

When congregations or worship committees debate whether they should retain such treasured liturgical touchstones as the Lord's Prayer or the words of institution in the context of communion, they are often asking the wrong questions to begin with, as well as offering solutions to those wrongly put questions.

So often conversations center around "relevance," "reaching out to seekers," and "avoiding rote repetition." Each one of these concerns has validity in and of itself. Who would doubt that we indeed seek to be relevant and fresh in the midst of a community that is hospitable to seekers? We most certainly do. The way to get there, however, is not by jettisoning liturgical material that is either historic or repetitive. Much of the most historic worship material we share is actually more "relevant" than its weaker alternatives.

For instance, the reason that it is so important to say the Lord's Prayer by heart, over and over again, is that it has sufficient power and staying power to speak universally in timeless ways. The same might be said of the *Prayer of Saint Francis*, "Lord, make me an instrument of your peace," or the sixteenth-century prayer from the *Sarum Primer* that has become a liturgical fixture in one of the worship services in my own community, "God be in my head and in my understanding." These are highly relevant, historic pieces of tradition that often make eyes glisten with tears when they are shared.

The same might be said about repetition. The fact that something is repeatable does not minimize its importance. Meals, for instance, are repeated, and I am grateful that they are. When your stomach is growling a repeated meal is appreciated. I just love hot, freshly baked, buttered bread. It was good yesterday, and it will be better right now. It is precisely the quality of repetition that allows us to remember why we treasure it so.

When Milan Kundera wrote his intriguing novel *The Unbearable Lightness of Being* (HarperCollins, 1984), he played with the concept of being and repetition. Nothing, prodded Kundera, has enough gravity, weight, and staying power to last if it passes through our field of perception but once. It is simply too light and will float away. Only repetition provides continuity enough and weight enough to satisfy memory and meaning.

Many things bear repeating: eat your vegetables; look both ways before you cross the street; a penny saved is a penny earned. Some things bear repeating often: Happiness is a by-product of right living; give more than you receive; this too shall pass. Moreover, a few things bear repeating always: The Lord is my Shepherd, I shall not want; forgive us our sins as we forgive those who sin against us; this is my body broken for you.

The fact that something is either historic or repeated does not automatically define it as irrelevant. Exactly the opposite may be true. Because it has stood the test of time, it may be sufficiently deep to allow me to swim more deeply in it. Because it is repeated, I have another chance, today, to go where I could not go yesterday.

To be sure, all traditions must constantly be reassessed, but this reassessment must not be based on false assumptions. The real question has to do with *how* the ecumenical historic pattern of the liturgy, including treasures from the tradition, is represented to the worshiping community. How might insights from postmodern awareness project the ecumenical historic shape of the liturgy with a metalanguage?

CHAPTER SEVEN

Betwixt and Between

Worship and Liminal Reality

In the year that King Uzziah died, I saw the Lord sitting on a throne, high and lofty; and the hem of his robe filled the temple.

ISAIAH 6:1

It was from anthropologists that we first heard about it; broad patterns of cultural transition and regeneration are ushered forward by *rites of passage*. These rites allow social systems and individual persons to mediate powerful changes within their ranks. These transitions include the normal and expected ones, such as departure from childhood and betrothal, but they also include dire times of crisis, such as war and death.

What Arnold van Gennep and then Victor Turner identified was a category of being that was in between. It was the inner domain of a rite of passage and transition, and they called it the *liminal* domain. What is characteristic of this state of being is its position in relation to structure. Liminal reality is that space and time that has broken with prevailing structure, whatever that may be. Precisely because it is positioned between the structures of life, it holds latent power for future transformation.

In the first phase of transition, *separation,* there is a time of breaking with the old. This may be voluntary or involuntary, depending on circumstance. In the last phase of transition, there is a time of *reaggregation* or reentry. This ushers one back into the world of structure, though not in the same state one was before the transition. In between this entrance and exit is the liminal time itself.

Preliminal ▶ ‖   **Liminal**   ‖ ▶ Postliminal
        ⬆   ⬆
   separation   reaggregation

This betwixt and between time is filled with ambiguity. It lacks past coordinates and familiar form. The person who is moving through this time is a liminal person—a transitional person—and ritually unsafe to the rest of the community. Rituals are necessary to assure the transition and keep the individual person and the community secure. It is common for individual persons who pass through a liminal time with others to develop a special camaraderie that Turner coined as *communitas.* It is a bond that transcends all socially constructed distinctions. Good examples of *communitas* might include those who survived a crisis together or served in the military during the same time of war.

For many this time of liminal passage represents a symbolic form of death and rebirth. The old passes away, and the new is born—a new self, a new status, a new form of existence. As such, the liminal domain is one fraught with possibility for transformation. The character of transforming liminal reality is best described as one that holds an aspect of sacred time and space.

Liminal existence is located in designated, separated *sacred space*. Isaiah finds himself in the presence of the Lord in the temple of holiness (Isa. 6:1–6), and Jacob's dream floats somewhere in the sacred axis between heaven and earth (Gen. 28:12–19). *Sacred time* takes place as persons and communities are separated from ordinary chronology and the meanings that it holds.

Mircea Eliade places the locus of the revelation of sacred knowledge in the center of the sacred time and space continuum. Liminal time and space are just such a locale, the preeminent setting in which revelation takes place, knowledge is imparted, and consciousness changed.

For Christians, these patterns are not unfamiliar. In a liminal moment between the old self and the new one, the initiate plunges into the watery chaos of baptism, reemerging a new person in Christ and with the beloved community (Rom. 6:1–14). This new state of being is shared in *communitas* with others who have experienced this same transition as they share the same ritual food (1 Cor. 12:12–27). All drink of the same spirit, part of the same body of Christ (Gal. 3:27–28).

Corporate worship, at its best, can be understood as a liminal domain of sacred time and space that is set over and against the ongoing structure of life. A special *communitas*, or *koinonia*, exists among those who gather; and liturgical symbols, sacred speech, and ritual acts define it as a transforming locale. The locale of liminal transformation is bounded by sacred time and space, which are provided and shepherded by a ritual leader who has designated authority within the community and its tradition.

The worshiping community enters into this liminal reality by means of a pilgrimage. Personal preparation may include special dress or a familiar route to the place of worship. Corporate rituals of entry and preparation may include prayers, ceremonial washing, or symbolic acts. The entry into the sacred space is almost always through a symbolic threshold, portal, or door (Lat: limen = threshold). The place of worship is different by design. Its architecture projects sacred meanings, and it is filled with symbols, arrangements of objects, and special art or icons. In a minimalist move, it may also *remove* many of the ordinary objects of life in order to make it a space radically different from the rest of material life.

The place of worship is like a clay pot holding treasure. It is the destination of pilgrimage and the eventual departure place for return. The pilgrimage dimension of liminal time and space parallels that of the ecumenical-historic pattern of worship. It requires entrance into a sacred space, a time of transformation, and the eventual sending back into the world to serve:

Entrance▶ Word▶ Table▶ Sending▶
Preliminal ‖ .... Liminal .... ‖ Postliminal

CHAPTER EIGHT

The Metaworship Labyrinth

Pilgrims on the Postmodern Path

*Your word is a lamp to my feet
and a light to my path.*

PSALM 119:105

As a rediscovered prayer practice, the ancient form of the labyrinth has assumed renewed importance as a pathway to increased spiritual depth and awareness. The walking of a labyrinth can lead the pilgrim not only through time and space but also to places inaccessible to routine perception. Although one encounters radical twists and turns on the way, the labyrinth—unlike its cousin the maze—invariably leads to the center. It is not designed to fool or mislead, but rather to transport its guests to different states of being. This does not mean, however, that a labyrinth walker may travel mindlessly. On the contrary, one must remain alert to what may be revealed and the ways in which mind, body, and spirit might be unified.

You are invited to walk imaginitively through the following labyrinth and to think of each turn you make as a powerful point at which the metaworship principles we explore in this chapter (Sacred Space, Word Enacted, Room for Mystery) shape transforming worship. You may come to realize that, just as when you walk a labyrinth, each newly found awareness frequently leads to another one.

Sacred Space

In the same way that special attention was given to the furnishings of the nomadic tabernacle, the architecture of the temple, or for that matter the provisions of the Last Supper, so careful attention is required in the preparation of all sacred space. From the simplest Quaker meeting house to Chartres cathedral in France, the space in which we meet is sacramental, the outward and visible sign of an inward and spiritual grace. *How* we adorn and use this set-apart space will determine the ways in which the space will be transformative.

We now pause for a Protestant phobia alert:

"Attention: Will a Mr. J.Q. Protestant please come to the service desk? Your children have lost you."

"Yes, I am J.Q."

"I'm afraid the children of your movement have become so afraid of creating external idols that they have developed some rather severe phobias."

"Such as?"

"Such as the fear of lighting candles. Incense is almost an impossibility."

"I'm afraid that's the way the icons crumble. So what do you want from me?"

"We're sorry to inform you, Mr. Protestant, but you are being placed under house arrest immediately."

"What? You can't do that!"

"Oh yes we can…at least until their world is once again open to material, earthy, sacramental, sensory pathways of worship."

As he is led away, his descendants look, as it were, with new eyes into the face of multisensory worship. It isn't that flowers somehow are spontaneously growing out of the cracks in the sanctuary mortar, but already the possibilities begin to present themselves.

Liminal worship space, sacred time and space, goes on-line with all senses activated: sight, sound, smell, taste, and touch. Be not afraid, you may light as many candles as you like until the end of the age.

Threshold

As we prepare for the worship theme of "the race," we ask ourselves, "How will people know that they have entered a race in coming here, that life is a race, that our faith is a race to the finish line with God?" To mark the threshold and worship space we use a visual image that captures the sense of motion, of human motion, stretching toward the completion. It is a silhouette of three runners. "I have run the race." Indeed, Paul, you have, and we do.

The image is enlarged to many sizes—large poster size, smaller tabletop models, handheld half-sheets. Large images are posted at every entrance to the church and then again as people walk through the foyer on the way to the sanctuary. Our mission: Make it impossible for any person to cross into worship space without colliding with this image. It hangs down halfway in front of the sanctuary doors so that one has to duck or go around it to enter.

Once inside, the worshiper sees the image projected on two screens to the left and right, and it is the cover art for bulletins. Music is playing. Can it be? No, tell me not: theme music with some familiar Olympian motif? It's subconscious, of course. Who was that who broke the record in the one-hundred-yard dash?

This is a different time and space, and it is not operating according to the logic of other time and space. The church has taken it over. It belongs to the church this morning, and it has a purpose. This isn't your father's *chronos*; it's *kairos*, God's time.

The chosen music for the day has to do with journey, pilgrimage, homecoming, race, and striving. The final blessing is the Irish one, "May the road rise to meet you, may the wind be always at your back."

For the service of the Word, the pastor tells the scripture from the epistle and then begins describing how the Greeks celebrated the Olympics. So many allusions to the games are found in letters written in that culture. How is it that Paul took the raw stuff of his culture and created gospel with it? Do you remember that scene from *Chariots of Fire* in which the main character refused to run on the Sabbath? What was all *that* about?

The pastor stops. One of the members of the congregation, who has just run a marathon, rises and tells his story. He especially describes what it is like to "hit the wall" near the end, just before you find your second wind. It seems impossible, but then it comes—a burst from beyond.

That's how it is, says the pastor, when grace plunges in on the world. All our efforts lean on it, are fueled by it, are saved by it. Thank God there is a table for us in this race of faith. Thank God for bread and wine and fellow travelers. We're so exhausted, so tired, but so, so thankful. The gifts of God for the people of God.

Go run the race. Fed and filled. You're not alone. Until we meet again.

This is meant to be outrageous time and space for God and God's people.

Palette

In much of the Protestant worship world, color was limited to the green and red tones of Christmas—borrowed, we might add, from wrapping paper schemes and commercial storefront displays—and from the spring pastels of Easter egg baskets.

Throw an Easter lily or two in, and you have some white too. The liturgical renewal movement brought several space-oriented accents with it: the church year and its colors and banners, banners, banners. The question now for most is *not* "Should we use color? How about banners?" but "*How* do we use color, and in what *ways* can fabrics be used in the service of worship?"

The church year is itself a form of alternate time—not based on either the seasons or a secular calendar. It has its own internal logic and is based on, of all things, a story, an alternative story alongside the dominant story of our culture. It takes a leap to say that the first Sunday of Advent is the beginning of our repeating family story, but for those who enter into this strange time world, a metanarrative keeps running like a background music track to the drama of the world's life.

This church year has its own colors, symbols, textures, and buoyancies. It rises and falls with its story. From anticipation to fulfillment, the course leads us through familiar, repeating terrain. How do we know the season has changed?

On the first Sunday of Advent, the congregation walks into a worship space in which large spans of plain purple fabric reach from altar to nave, across the ceiling, in broad arcs of motion. It seems as though the purple spews out of the Holy of Holies and pours out on worshipers. It is the invasion of Advent, and no one can miss it. Added to that is the relocated communion table, now centered at the foot of the chancel steps, swathed with hues of purple. Votive candles are ubiquitous. A voice from the rear of the sanctuary: "O Come, O Come Emmanuel." It is the ancient, mournful, mysterious chant. The new people notice that long-timers scarcely need their hymnals. What is this dark expectation? Can it be named?

What are absent are banners with lots of words on them, glued on felt with loving hands. Walls of words do not a postmodern space make. What *is* present is ambient light, movement of fabric, colors with their connotations and the symbols and signs of a hope you can almost taste. We have walked *into* Advent instead of only teaching about it. The church is clothed in Advent, and though the lessons and message, hymns and songs will most surely tell the story, the people have *become* the story too.

The Red People. Pentecost used to be the best-kept secret, but not any more. Now we talk about the coming of the Spirit. That means that the body of Christ is ablaze with red on this day. Not only are brightly colored banner poles covered with orange, red, and yellow streamers. Not only is the altar striped with the kind of primary colors that make you want to say, "Where *is* my painting apron?" Not only is there a free span of fabric pennants that reach down from the ceiling toward the worshipers like tongues of flame. The people of God have worn red, so they are the swirling insides of the outsides of the church.

There was a sound like a mighty wind on that Pentecost—and so there is here too. The synthesized sounds of wind and storm fade into the introduction of the first song. It will be impossible to come forward for communion without stumbling over the large basin in the center, a font in which the people of God will touch the waters and remember their baptisms. When the pastor introduces the baptismal remembrance, water is poured from one jug into the basin from some altitude—at least three feet—so the sound of pouring water is heard throughout the congregation. This is really what water sounds like when it is poured, and we are really baptized.

Glass

Stained-glass windows still tell the old-old, new-new story. Some of the newest sacred applications of glass are stunning in their movement, design, and ability to capture the essence of a story episode. The way they differ today is often the way much art differs from its antecedents; it is not representational, but more abstract. What is communicated is the feeling, the tension, the paradoxes as much as one-to-one descriptions. If the presented story is the woman at the well, for instance, then the object of reflection may be nothing more than her bucket and multifarious symbols for living water.

If postmodern changes are reflected artistically in the new glass, what is happening in its electronic equivalent, the digitally projected image? All too often the procurers of the digital revolution continue to produce seventeenth- to nineteenth-century concepts with twenty-first–century technology. Not all digital projection is the same, and there is a qualitative difference between postmodern and modern presentations *using the same equipment.*

I remember one of my first efforts at projecting a sermon "aid" up on a screen during a worship service. I asked a new college graduate, one who majored in public relations and advertising, what she thought. I expected rave reviews for trying such an innovative thing, but they were not forthcoming. She said, "Honestly? It really didn't do anything for me. Kind of distracting, really. Reminded me of the kind of things you see in a college classroom these days, or in one of my company meetings. A bunch of PowerPoint® stuff saying what they told you. Like, you think we didn't get it when you told us? It's like an electronic flannel board. You feel that you have to impress us with a trendy outline?"

"Really," she concluded, "I don't come to church for that." And she doesn't. In fact, that kind of thing is often the source of embarrassment among the Millennials. It's certainly not anything they want their friends to see or to associate with *their* church. Their Boomer parents try hard to use technology to impress, to show how with it they are, but the Millennials remain unimpressed with Boomer efforts for good reason; they are already hyper-technological. Such bells and whistles are of no interest—they can get that anywhere, but better.

Isn't it time to declare a moratorium on PowerPoint® presentations and bullet-point self-improvement sermons? Words on screens for singing present another practical matter that involves getting heads up and out of printed materials, but let's not fool ourselves—this is no postmodern invention.

After all, how more print-culture could it be? *Words, words, words* projected on a megawhite board.

Then what? Pictures, images, icons, yes. But not canned and corny. Stay away from the greeting card effect. Think in terms of video montages: choose pictures, symbols, and art that capture raw experience; ambiguity and unresolved tensions; faces on the other side of the world or next door; mysterious, untamed natural beauty; ancient things and yesterday's front page; all the deep, perplexing, mysterious symbols that people have been trying so hard to get rid of.

In recent visits to the Taizé community in France and the Christian Fellowship Church in Belfast, Northern Ireland, I experienced the power of sacred space in wildly contrasting contexts and pieties.

The contemplative Taizé worship is full of silence, chanting, and simple readings. The participants are seated on the floor, surrounding the inner community of monks. There is no written liturgy. Worshipers have a songbook. Prompts are given by cantors and readers who are largely out of sight. The front of the Reconciliation Chapel is bathed in candlelight, full of icons, and covered with upswept fabric. An odor of holiness pervades the gathered community. Three times a day the Spirit circles the enclave and burrows into longing or unsuspecting victims. Few are left unchanged. They often return for more.

The nonpartisan, neopentecostal, socially active Christian Fellowship Church of East Belfast, Northern Ireland, is abuzz with conversation and music the moment you enter its building. Children and young families are everywhere. Musicians are preparing to play. Informal conversations are scattered across the floor. This Vineyard-influenced congregation is reaching into its community in powerful ways. Ministry tables line the rear of the worship area and offer explanations for everything from their mission in East Belfast—the Oasis Coffee Shop— to healing and reconciliation prayer services for the troubled areas of the city. The service begins as the band assembles onstage, and the youth choir members take their places. Words are projected on a screen, and the music begins. The congregation sings songs of praise to God as banner carriers swirl their multicolored banners up and down the aisles. During the prayer time, worshipers are invited to come forward and pick up a small gold-colored bead to take with them, to remind them of the treasure that they carry. They are invited to touch their fingers in oil and then to their eyes as a reminder of sacred sight. Those who desire prayer receive the laying on of hands.

These are two extremely different worship experiences, but both drink deeply of the Spirit of God. Do they reflect different spiritual and emotional longings? Yes and no. The pathways are certainly different in form. One could argue that the brain itself is engaged in different ways in these two services, but the same God breaks through.

Both use sacred space remarkably well. Both create a multisensory experience. Both experience eternity symbolized in an alternate locale in which souls and communities are transformed. In both cases, the holy ground is unmistakable.

Word Enacted

When John the seer described the heavenly court of his apocalyptic vision, it was with incomparable drama that he did so. How else could one paint a word picture of the heavenly

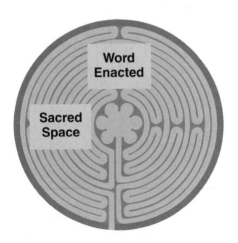

host adoring and worshiping God and the Lamb without ceasing? It was not a stage play, dramatization, or skit that he was presenting; the movement of his saga was *itself* dramatic. That was its character. So is the best worship we share this side of eternity.

In the same way that the being and love of God are always incarnated in the movement of history, so the story, convictions, truth, and beauty that we know through the gospel are embodied in the worship of the people of God. Yahweh continues to be enthroned on the praises of Israel. The body of Christ carries resurrection power into the world. In the container of sacred space that belongs to God, we move and act in parallel to the heavenly court. "Thy will be done on earth, as it is in heaven." The people of God live out the unseen in time and space.

When the children of Israel approached the threshold of the temple, they prepared themselves by the singing of psalms. These psalms of ascent anticipated the holiness to which they were heading. "Who shall ascend the hill of the LORD? And who shall stand in his holy place?" (Ps. 24:3). The entrance is marked with songs of praise and thanksgiving: "Let us come into his presence with thanksgiving; let us make a joyful noise to him with songs of praise!" (Ps. 95:2). The people stand and lift holy hands to their maker.

What characterizes the journey of worshiping pilgrims from the first to the last is dramatic, sacred movement. From the joyful procession and gathering in praise, to the trek to the altar for prayer or communion, to the blessed return to the world, the people of God move in their bodies, minds, and spirits toward God. They enter into the story and then become it.

The locale of the drama is sacred space. These worshipers, these in-between, liminal people are the actors in this altered time and space. The grand biblical story is the strangely written libretto. The ordained ministers are combination actors, directors, truth-tellers, and complex symbols, and God...God is both producer and active partner. The drama is about God's love affair with the world, from beginning to end, and God is no passive audience. The Spirit intercedes with sighs too deep for words (Rom. 8:26).

In *en-acted* worship, every entrance, lighting of a candle, setting of the altar, or bringing of the fire of presence needs to be purposeful, intentional, and loaded with symbolic freight. En-acted worship must be multisensory and engage them all— sight, sound, smell, taste, and touch. Even *holding* a hymnal is an experience of memory and touch. It brings powerful associations and memories. Tasting communion bread and smelling the fragrance of a familiar worship space are experiences appealing to memory, taste, and smell. The sight of the ordained pastor entering sacred space and pausing to regard the cross brings connotations with every minister ever known. This is the set-apart one, a walking, living, breathing symbol.

Rule of thumb: When it can be dramatized, symbolized, and enacted instead of your simply giving a verbal explanation—do it.

When the act of child dedication or baptism takes place, use oral tradition in telling the story of Mary and Joseph presenting their son, Jesus, at the temple. Ask for important commitments from parents. Encourage the congregation to stand and enter into the covenant along with them. Create a chain of prayer from the congregation all the way to the child, one in which everyone is touching. Make it happen in time and space.

I recently attended a ceremony that a scouting program hosted for its young people who were passing from childhood to adolescence. It was obvious how they marked the rite of passage with all the senses. It was also clear how easily the loosely related parents and attendees entered into this countercultural drama.

The metanarrative of the scouting program draws on quasi-religious, quasi-Native American themes. Ceremonial incense of sage and cedar was lit. The lights in the room were lowered. Along with other signs of encampment, an imitation campfire accented the ceremony area. Ceremonial drums were pounding both before and during the ritual. Then, when it was time to recognize the initiates, "tribal elders" came forward, wearing ritual clothing and makeup. Their role was to usher the young into the next phase. Each young person was summoned forward, marked with ceremonial paint in symbols that were interpreted—each one connoting a different virtue necessary for courageous and compassionate adulthood. They were then escorted over a low bridge, leaving one shore of life in order to cross over to the next.

Here was an assembly of relative strangers, at the most acquaintances, willingly participating in a culturally artificial rite that was imported from outside their normal repertoire of language and behavior. Nevertheless, the rite of passage had meaning for both the young people and their attending relatives. It was highly intentional. It smacked of tradition. It was related to a referent beyond itself. It was essentially communal. It had clear ritual leadership, and it was highly effective.

If a culturally borrowed rite can have an impact on a group of people with very contingent commitments—limited mostly to a short window of time in which their children are eligible for the program—what might happen if those who are baptized into the body of Christ and are united in the Spirit took the drama, ceremony, rites, and rituals of our tradition with equal seriousness? How much more the revolutionary story of the gospel deserves it. What a difference could be created in the worship of the people of God because of it.

It is the Saturday night before Easter Sunday. The baptismal candidates enter a darkened church and meet their mentors and pastors by candlelight. These adults have worked with them for weeks, discussing the faith, sharing life, and being living witnesses. Now they are ushering them through the ancient watch night, the Easter Vigil, the night before Resurrection Sunday.

As a group, they are led around the darkened church, one candle before and one following. Their journey takes them to different rooms in the church, where different parts of the sacred story are read. By the running water of the chapel fountain, they hear the words, "In the beginning…" Down they go to the boiler room, only to hear words from the psalm, "De profundus!" Out of the depths, the belly of the earth, the voice comes. They climb the narrow stairwell up to the top of the church tower, where the pictures of the saints, some living, but mostly gone, are on display. Each face is examined by only the flicker of the candle. They lived, loved, built churches, had families, taught classes, baptized, worshiped, ate together, and shared all the profound passages of life together. A great cloud of witnesses.

The initiates are taken to a holding area where they wait with their mentors. The pastors disappear and then return to retrieve each candidate and accompanying mentor by name. One by one, they walk into the darkened sanctuary and are seated in silence on the floor of the chancel. The candidates form an inner circle, and their mentors form an outer circle around them. Finally, after each person is ferried to the holy place, there is silence. Out of the silence comes prayers of the pastors for the dynamic process that has brought them to this place. Mentors lay hands on the shoulders of the young candidates sitting in front of them and pray for them by name. All close with the Lord's Prayer, holding hands.

The passage ends as they are escorted back to where they began, anticipating the coming of the next morning. Such is the transformational waiting of the tomb before the stone is rolled away.

Will they remember every word that was spoken during this rite of passage? I am afraid not. What they will know and remember is that they passed through a mystery on the way to transformation. From heart to mind to body, they know that surely God was in this place.

It is Christmas Eve. The worship space is bathed in the light of candles. During the service of the Word, a story is told and local tradition enacted: The pastor, holding a single candle, tells the birth narrative from Luke by heart. There is a grand pause, everyone waits, and then the words begin, "In those days a decree went out from Caesar Augustus that all the world should be enrolled."

It is the first Sunday after September 11. The heavyhearted flock crawls into worship. Some are clutching their chests, trying to breathe. Others are clenching their teeth. Still others are already clenching their fists. There are some strange faces in the larger than usual crowd this morning, but as on Easter and Christmas, the crowd swells mostly because the every Sunday, every-other Sunday, and once-a-month worshipers all show up at the same time.

The choir processes in without singing, during the prelude. A small, simple altar has been added to the chancel area. It is set with a lone rose and a flag. It is unusual for this congregation to have a national symbol so centrally located, but this is no usual Sunday. It is a time for lament for many reasons.

A trio of cello, classical guitar, and Irish tin whistle accompany a lone voice that sings, "Come to me, O weary traveler; come to me in your distress; come to me, you heavy burdened; come to me and find your rest." As the song proceeds, a solitary woman moves slowly up the aisle. She is dressed in black and holds a black cloth draped over her arm. By the time she has arrived in the chancel area, the words of the song are, "Do not fear, my yoke is easy; do not fear, my burden's light; do not fear the path before you; do not run from me in fright."

The woman sways to the mournful sound of lament. Every face in the congregation beholds the story she is shaping with a sacrifice of her own body. Slowly, as the song draws to a close, the cello drones its final melody line; the woman covers the altar with the shroud and melts to her knees. She stays there the longest time. No one moves. No one utters a sound. All has been said by saying nothing.

En-act the powerful, life-giving, world-shattering, logic-defying Word. The whole worship experience is one of motion, dramatic movement through time, God's time, to transform. Are we pilgrims going somewhere?

En-acted worship balances rational, word-centered, print-dominated worship. It appeals to the senses and aesthetics. En-acted worship does not separate what one knows about God from the experience of God's mystery. Ritual is the lingua franca of the worshiping people, and symbol is the currency of its community. Because everyone can participate on some level, in some way, no one is left as a passive observer. At the center of en-acted worship lies the feast of incarnation—the Word become flesh, known by an actual feast of bread and wine.

Eat it. Reflect on it. Eat it again.

Go ahead, move, but move intentionally. Find an excuse for the choir to process and recess. Add in children. Host prayer paths punctuated by meditation stations. Base Good Friday on the Via Dolorosa and stop at each agonizing place along the way. Walk the entire congregation through the stations of the cross. Have a tithing march. Walk a labyrinth. Light it with candles, flood it with ethereal music, and precede it with ancient history of the prayer discipline. March the congregation single file to the time capsule and open it ceremonially. Have the oldest and youngest members of the body reveal its contents with great surprise and flourish, one artifact at a time. Understand how to proclaim the truth visually and through our bodies.

In all this, leadership matters, of course. Although the whole people of God do the *liturgia,* the work of the people, ritual leadership by the spiritual leaders of the community is indispensable. The ordained ministers of the community are the central sign of continuity with the church of the ages and the church universal. Their presence alone is symbolic, in and of itself—loaded with complex identity and role. The *way* in which they preside, however, leads the whole community to particular worshiping ends.

Is the ritual leader's leadership *purposeful, graceful, and focused on God?*

To lead with purpose is to do just that; the pastor must move with a knowing strength:

We are in your holy place, O God, reciting holy mysteries, and sharing holy things. These hungry people have come for bread. I know where they shall it and rejoice in pointing to that mystery. I know my purpose in being here today, and I would rather be here, sharing in this experience, than anywhere else on the planet.

To lead with grace is to know that nothing we do proceeds without the love of God behind it:

It is grace and grace alone that calls me to lead on your behalf, my God. I am filled with humility and awe that you might use a broken vessel such as me to gather the beloved community together. Let me be an avenue of the same power that you have given me. Let the love of Christ flow out through me so that others may know the riches of your grace.

To lead in the spirit is to know that God is the beginning and end of all our reflection, praise, and love:

Help me to move among your people without self-preoccupation. Let me not be swayed by either criticism or praise, or respond too quickly to the demand for personal preference from your children. Above all, help me surrender to you by forgetting myself. Let every action of my leading point beyond myself, a voice in the wilderness proclaiming that you are the Lord of our highest love.

Like the rest of en-acted worship, the proclamation of the preacher should be evocative, based in narratives, move from print-culture to oral culture, and incarnated in the being of the gospel teller. This is not an occasion for delivering a manuscript, providing book reports on self-help books, or impressing the flock with theological gymnastics. This is thoughtful sacred speech that draws pilgrims to the throne of grace. The earthy, incarnational intersection of the Story with the hopes and fears of all the years—our stories—is the world-creating, oppression-destroying, community-building, hope-casting fruit of faithful preaching. Above all, it leaves room for the hearer to unpack the "what next" of the gospel in his or her culture, context, life situation, worldview, and emerging theology. It is the free gospel, and it may fly and live without our attempts to overcontrol it.

This en-acting community, in sacred space, with faithful proclamation, makes for a deep hospitality. More than friendly, it rests on a transformation beyond niceness. All of the strangers have been invited. This table is truly large enough.

Room for Mystery

Advent question: How do you look forward to something that has already happened? For example, how do you observe the coming of Jesus when he has already come? Answer: Wrong question. Live with the paradox. You're waiting forever for something that has eternally come. Keep on waiting; you can't reconcile it in your mind. So stop trying and keep telling the story anyway. You'll get it someday.

In the same way that explaining the punch line of a good joke destroys it, so wrongly placed *overexplaining* destroys the

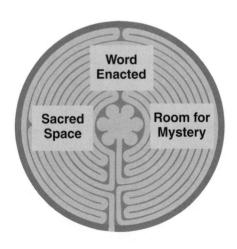

veracity of the truth that sustains us. As Bernard of Clairvaux retorted to his rival contemporary Anselm of Canterbury—one who felt the need to explain every *why* of what should be accepted by faith and known intuitively—*let mystery be mystery*. It is not that truth should not be explicated, conceptualized, and related to the rest of scripture, tradition, and such things as ethics and practice—of course it frequently should be. Rather, there is a tender margin that cannot be known through rationality alone. Some things can only be known through adoration and wonder. This is not just a gap of incomprehensibility because we have not yet discovered it. It is a *permanent* hiddenness.

For those who practice a strict rationalism, leaving a wide margin of mystery is a risky kind of business, a perceived chink in the empirical armor. After all, shouldn't the system be consistent, logical from beginning to end, without seam or interruption?

This false dichotomy actually contains two complementary poles. For those who have a rigorously intellectual faith, the recognition of mystery only completes human knowing; humility overcomes pride—knowing what can't be known. This deep humility and awe strikes one mute in the face of beauty, infinity, depth, healing, suffering, and the seemingly impossible.

In the same way, a holistic theology and worship provides room for both high praise and deep lament. There is ample room for both in a dynamic worship. The practice of silence is just such a way to recognize mystery.

Because Protestant worship has frequently resembled a house of words, the presence of silence often appears as an unwelcome guest. When silence knocks on the front door, we may be willing to go so far as exchanging cordial niceties on the front porch. What we may not be willing to do is to invite it into the front room for lemonade and extended conversation. Like the stranger, silence often disarms us and our well-constructed defenses.

Silence deserves the status of honored guest among God's people. We can set aside intentional time for silence not only in collective prayer but also as a creative response to the proclaimed Word, the afterglow of the Lord's table, and in other numerous occasions to ponder the imponderable.

Now, in the empty space below and on the next page, pause for sixty seconds of silence to listen, watch, wait, and reflect on what you have just been reading:

Skipped it, didn't you? Do you secretly assume that the *real* importance is to be found in what is written next, rather than in the silence? If so, you are to be numbered among the sands of the oceans. We transfer this same attitude, this way of perceiving, to worship. Silence is experienced as something to move through quickly or to be avoided. I am not referring to the awkward pauses in worship flow that are the result of poor planning, inadequately prepared leadership, or some technological glitch. No, I mean the avoidance of deep silence itself, the passing over of silence.

Think now about the frenetic pace and content of our present sound bite, wired world. Think, too, about the thousands of young people who are at this very moment longing, searching, and finding places of mystery and silence. Imagine what can be offered to them, and by extension, to the whole church. Imagine scores of young adults not having to turn away from the church to find the mystery of faith. Imagine them discovering it within our own tradition.

Many young people today are drawn to silence, prayer, and contemplation. They long for a mysterious counterpoint to the white noise and speed of light information overload of their times. What is so deep that it cannot be captured in a sea of propositions? Where is an outer environment that sends me to inner space? How can I transcend the crush of time with the timeless?

Because the modern worldview maintains a tacit rejection of any supernatural dimensions of reality, the ubiquitous biblical portraits of healing and even exorcism are summarily dismissed, or at the least explained away. Yet throughout the world today, phenomena such as healing are commonplace. This is to be found not only in premodern cultures in which supernatural elements are understood to be part of the way reality exists but also alongside the materialism of scientific modernity.

The worldview that does not permit the unexplainable is now itself being questioned, indeed, is questioning its own presuppositions. Medical establishments across the country are now providing viable roles for the intersection of medicine and religious healing. The churches—the mothers of such practices in the past—are only now reclaiming what has been lost. Healing services are reemerging out of the shadows of the church's own history.

Go ahead, anoint with oil and pray for healing. Lay on hands, and seek deliverance from all that binds.

All this is not hard to find. In fact, it is stitched into the lining of the gospel. Simply reclaim it for worship:

Expose the symbolic.

Allow time for paradox and ambiguity.

Encourage mystery to remain what it is.

Don't overexplain.

Give equal time to the nonrational.

Reclaim silent spaces.

Entertain the possibility of unexplainable healing.

CHAPTER NINE

9/11 Now and Then

Worship and Crisis

*Then I saw a new heaven and a new earth; for the first
heaven and the first earth had passed away.*

REVELATION 21:1

People instinctively gather together in times of crisis. This
is perhaps the enduring residue of a collective survival instinct;
we naturally band together for strength, protection, and
consolation in the face of loss, threat, and calamity. Turning to
the tribe is perhaps the most natural reaction to the shattering
of ordinary life. At least for a while, a new bond is forged
between those who have shared disasters small and large.
Unlikely relationships are born between allies who share strange
circumstances. Leaders are granted an unusual degree of
authority. Plans that only a short time before seemed stalled,

motionless, and impossible suddenly take wing. How? The temporary power of crisis.

If a native human response to crisis is to band together for survival, an equally important impulse is to make sense of what is often senseless. In circumstances such as these, people gather together not only for political debate in order to remedy or to provide the illusion of remedying a problem but also in candlelight vigils to pray and to hear edifying discourses that interpret the impossible. People wait breathlessly for a single well-worded sentence on which the experience might be hung. Many people turn to faith, even dormant faith. Such experiences often serve as the fodder of sacred disclosure.

From the moment the airliners crashed into the World Trade Center towers, the nation was ushered into an unrepeatable, involuntary liminal state of gigantic proportion. The physical carnage was paralleled by the emotional wreckage of victims, families, and fellow citizens. A dividing line had been crossed, and people knew—even in a state of shock—that some things could never be the same again.

Special services and observances were hastily convened. Once half-filled churches now swelled with row upon row of confused people who were praying, listening, and waiting. For what were they looking? How would religious communities respond?

To be sure, fearful people were looking for reassurance. Some were searching for a temporary crutch until they found their misplaced equilibrium, but there was more at work than that.

Faithful people instinctively turned to the heart of life, the guiding center of their faith. After all, if a religious tradition cannot speak in such a critical time, does it deserve to be taken seriously in any other time?

Imagine a time immediately after some defining crisis. The crowds come. The doors of the church are open, and the pews are filled with regular faces and the faces of strangers. There is an expectancy that is palpable. It travels across the room like lightning arcing across the night sky. What will happen now? What can possibly be said? Does our gathering make any difference? Can God possibly speak now? In a time of crisis, the needs of the worshiping community are daunting and intense. Sensitive and insightful pastoral leadership is required to create and lead a truly transformative worship experience. Because the purpose of this very specific kind of worship is to turn to God and transport worshipers from despair to gospel hope, the liturgical event is best understood as a passage. At its heart this passage is more collective than individual. This kind of urgent travel needs several propulsion systems that act simultaneously.

Ritual Leadership and Surround-Sound Symbols

In the aftermath of 9/11, pastors across the country encountered an interesting phenomenon: Parishioners and the public alike accorded religious leaders greater authority, liberty to make decisions, and a place of prominence to be heard. People turned to their religious leaders for guidance and leadership.

There was also an awakening for pastors and other ecclesial leaders. Even those sleepy pastors who had been coasting toward retirement and their pensions for years rediscovered their reasons for being. At the root of this phenomenon was something far more powerful than individual personalities. It was the historic and symbolic pastoral role itself. This complex and multilayered role becomes nowhere more conspicuous than in a time of crisis.

In a sense, the pastor embodies an ancient role in the present, bearing the signs of a tradition larger than self. The pastor stands before the congregation, representing hundreds of years of ordained leadership as it parades through history. The importance of the individual person is diminished even as the collective identity is enlarged. This symbolic person takes on truly *sacramental* dimensions—an outward sign of something beyond, something hidden.

Whatever other aspects of ministry are embodied in the life of a present-day pastor—builder, missionary, manager, leader—the essential pastoral and priestly dimensions rise to the surface in times of crisis. This is precisely why it is incumbent on pastoral leaders to step forward and fill these distinctive roles.

There is always *the question of direction*. I remember a parishioner dropping by the church on the same day as the terrorist attacks on New York and Washington, D.C. His question was a simple one: "What are we going to do?" In the midst of chaos, people actually want to know what to do, even if that something is only gathering together to wait and pray.

In the face of threat, human beings *reach for security*. Men who never hug anybody melted into embraces with the clerical gown. Teenagers gravitated to ministers like never before. Perhaps this is a reflection of the infant's grasping of mother or father, a crying out for parents in the middle of the night. If so, it is not cause for apology; it is but the mirror image of children of the cosmos reaching for their God.

In addition to the symbolic freight of the pastoral role itself are the *symbols of faith found in sacred space*. Familiar places of worship, symbols familiar to the religious palette, and dramatic enactment of the faith all combine to reestablish the foundations of the spiritual universe.

On the very first night following the attacks, our congregation gathered for what so many others did—a service of prayer. The room was candlelit, and the pastors were attired in clerical robes. One of the most important things that happened was the most simple; the pastors walked silently to the chancel steps and knelt for an extended time of silent prayer. At this point, the congregants were on their knees whether or not they left their seats. They accompanied their leaders who led them to a ritual kneeling before God. The space in which they knelt was filled with symbols of the faith of the ages. Indeed, the room itself was filled with the memory of many other times of worship. They were surrounded by signs of the gospel, but they were not just searching for consolation and sure foundations.

There is also an immediate attempt to *make sense of the thick layers of cause and effect, deal with deep emotions, and reflect theologically.* With the lines of emotional defense lowered, worshipers lean forward to hear some word, *any* word from the shepherd. What shall be said?

Healing Homilies

At that moment, the power of the proclamation of the gospel and the leading of public prayer is surprisingly exposed. It erupts into the worship domain when the spoken word is crafted and presented in exceptionally sensitive pastoral terms. This requires many things, but at the least:

Name the reality that is in the room. The ritual leader and pastor must name the experience that is paramount in everyone's mind. What are the suffering, pain, and shock that we encounter? How did it happen? What is the effect on us now? Can this be painted in a few words or images? This description of our foe must occur before rushing to either an analysis of the problem or a prescription for the future. This honest sharing lends integrity to everything else that follows. It is particularly helpful in certain cases where incidents are covered with taboo or shame. Suicide is a case in point. Although descriptions must be sensitive, pastoral conversation and liturgy cannot proceed as though this death has occurred like any other death. It most certainly has not. That unspoken cloud is hovering over the minds and hearts of those who are grieving. "I was as shocked as any of you to hear not only *that* he died, but *how* his life was ended."

Don't rush too quickly to easy answers. The most difficult times of crisis are fraught with complexity. It is not only presumptuous to speak too quickly but also injurious. A premature theological solution stops the natural process of struggle on the way to truth. It is a mistake to jump too quickly to answers, especially easy answers. We must not speculate about the mice hiding in the basement as elephants roam the halls upstairs. Assumptions about the will of God, however well-intentioned, have the unique distinction of creating more destruction and unresolved anger toward God than about anything else imaginable. It is best to postpone some attempted explanations and conclusions, if indeed they are possible at all. Authentic questioning on the part of a pastoral leader gives courage to the one suffering to do the same. "We all have more agonizing questions than answers right now, which is exactly why we should be together."

Whereas we do not want to be too hasty in bringing forth premature answers early in the service, *neither should we be too tardy*. In the same way that honest wrestling on the part of the minister gives courage to the listener to do the same, so people also long for a word spoken from the standpoint of faith. They hope for a word of faith that dares to come into the situation, a word that contains at least one handle to which they may hold and from which they may in turn ask more questions. We must be timely in calling on the guiding narratives, images, metaphors, and symbols by which we live, breathe, and have our being. The sources are many and rich: scripture, historic confessions of faith, the Lord's Prayer, and the great and beloved hymnody of the church. All of these life-giving springs lead us toward hope, trust, and healing.

The end of the matter has to do with the future. There is no speaking of crisis and worship without it. So, as we head toward the end of this conversation about transforming worship, we must turn to its beginning. The answer, of course, is yet to be… in the future.

CHAPTER TEN

Leaning toward the Future

Reclaiming the Lost Trajectory of Worship

I have learned about dying by looking at two pictures
Bjorn Olinder needed to look at when he was dying:
a girl whose features are obscured by the fall of her hair,
planting a flower, and a seascape: beyond the headland, a
glimpse of immaculate sand that awaits our footprints.

MICHAEL LONGLEY

It is the power of the future, our sense of God's future, that is conspicuously absent from most mainline Protestant worship. This irreplaceable category of the future has often been ignored, lost, or abandoned, and this, I am convinced, is to the great detriment of the church and its worship. At its worst the conspiracy of silence about the future has created at least two things: on the one hand, a cult of traditionalism stuck in the past; on the other, an unrealistic expectation of what the present moment can deliver. Absent the future, both past and present are drained of their potency. Without the future, there can no meaning for history, no hope, no expectation, no emerging freedom, no creation, no conversion, no forgiveness, and no transformation. Without the future, there can only be a massive past that grinds to a halt in the fleeting nanosecond of the present.

Why the abandonment of the future, especially in worship? Except for Easter sermons—and sometimes not even then— and a season of anticipation like Advent—a season that is often really cast as foreplay for Christmas Day—where do we find the future in our liturgy?

The answer has to do with theological moves and how those moves have been mirrored in worship, which have then inevitably reshaped our theology.

It is not difficult to understand why we have quarantined the future to that bookshelf in the back room or the old cedar chest that holds our sentimental artifacts. Many intellectual currents and forms of piety have contributed to our displacement of the future. Like a forcible relocation, the future was exiled to a place of irrelevancy and even scorn, a silent land that often hosts few visitors.

One project of the Enlightenment was to reposition the meaning of the future in the efforts of humanity rather than God. Except for relatively small pockets of resistance, it succeeded. Anthropology replaced theology. One hallmark of radical existentialism, for instance, was to center any or all meaning in a self-created present. No meaning is to be found outside of this self-creation in the midst of absurdity. If meaning is based in only subjectively created human terms, and all notions of the future are really only projections of wishes, how can one speak of the future without cracking a dismissive smile?

If Marx substituted class struggle for the providence of God as the primary dynamic of history; if Freud replaced transcendence with the subconscious; if Darwin posited natural process in the place of divine intent; how can we possibly speak of God, history, and the future in the same sentence? By extension, how can we speak of hope?

This morning, as the waitress poured my coffee and asked what I would like for breakfast, I told her that I would like some light shed on the nature of future and hope. She paused and then said, "If I win the lottery and can leave this place, I'll let you know." I answered something like, "Well, that's one form of hope."

Her response, and not mine, is the one to notice. Although her sense of hope had no transcendent coordinate, except for perhaps a vague sense of fate, it clearly related to certain wishes within her present location. *I want a way out of here.* What was prominently missing, however, was something much larger than the lottery could ever provide.

Was history purely absurd for her, aside from random good luck that might bring relief? Could she say it was purposeful in any larger sense? Did it involve anything greater than herself or the lottery committee and a gamble?

These philosophical shifts within the modern era do not represent our only problem with God and the future.

There is also the real problem that sincere Christians have with eschatology. Although they may struggle with the same philosophical moves mentioned above, they also may be reacting against and distancing themselves from *particular forms of eschatology.* I know, because that is a part of my story too.

As I passed through high school and then college, I found myself surrounded by a particular theological worldview. Although it was not the theological world of my congregation, it was that of the religious world that surrounded me. From TV evangelists to Hal Lindsey's *The Late, Great Planet Earth* to an unusual college physics professor who fancied himself an armchair theologian, I was barraged with one version of Christian eschatology. My own church was too silent on the matter to be helpful. The only response of my religious community was to retreat from the issue in some hope that it might go away.

This silence of my church left me and others like me with two options: embrace the prevailing popular eschatology and notion of how God will act in the future or dismiss it and focus on other ethical or spiritual issues. I was simply not presented with interpretive alternatives. Therefore, like many others, I opted for shelving the future. Of that day and hour, not even the angels know. Lord, I certainly don't.

The same dilemma exists today for Christians who are exposed to monochromatic versions of Christian eschatology. The most notable is the *Left Behind* series, dressing up this theology in the fast-selling wardrobe of adventure fiction.

Not too long ago I ran into one of the lapsed members of my flock. He went on and on about this most recent incarnation of popular eschatology, not aware of any alternatives to it. He was insistent that this really shook him up. Upon asking him what this might mean for his life, he could only respond that he certainly didn't want to get left behind. However, our visit was cut short because he was on the way to purchase the next in his series of luxury-class sports cars, another toy for his collection. I suppose if one can drive fast enough, it is possible to *out-race* the future.

My problem, and I believe most people's problem with God and the future, was that the options were framed in exceedingly narrow terms: *Left Behind* theology or leave-it-all-alone theology. What I didn't know earlier in my life was that this one current of thought, this one apocalyptic scenario, this way of dividing up history into dispensations, is a very recent development in the history of Christian thought. Most certainly, end-time scenarios have emerged throughout the history of the church, often in times of social and personal crisis, but by and large, this apocalyptic eschatology has not been the dominant force of the church's reflection on the future.

It is of great concern, I believe, that our reaction against this one option has led us to leave behind *all* viable categories of the future in our theology and worship. This inclination is presently visible in biblical studies as Jesus' proclamation of the reign of God is sanitized of its future urgency: It's really only about social critique of the present. We *need* this baby, and it is too important to be thrown out with the bathwater. Theologians such as Pannenberg, Moltmann, and Cobb, have reminded us—each in his own way—that we must reclaim the future and its driving trajectory. It is time to lay aside our fears of or embarrassment with idiosyncratic apocalypticism. Language of the future must not continue to be monopolized and controlled by certain brands of American neoevangelicalism. We must not become silent because they speak loudly. In its varied forms, a robust theology of the future is encoded in the language of scripture. It is found in the historical confessions and liturgies of the ecumenical church. It is impossible to walk through the dim corridors of the catacombs on the Appian Way outside of Rome and not sense this urgent leaning toward the future. The art on those walls screams what we also find in the written texts of the same time, the ancient mantra of the church: "Maranatha, come Lord Jesus." Our language—especially our liturgical language—can once again embody this future urgency and expectation.

Why is it that Advent and Lent provide a sudden deepening to our worship that does not happen the rest of the church year? It is the *power of purple*; the way in which waiting and expectation function in worship. By their natures, the purple seasons prepare, wait, anticipate, and hope for the future moving of God. They actually wait for something that has already happened—incarnation or resurrection. For us, however, that drama is a repeating one; we always wait for incarnation and resurrection.

What if our worship began to embody this dynamic of purposeful waiting all the time, not only in Advent and Lent? What would happen if we actually came to believe that the reign of God is not only among us but also yet to be? How would this reshape our communities of faith as they struggle in the midst of crisis or suffering? How could the prophetic redescription of God's future create a new world? In what ways would the eucharist be transformed as we anticipate the fulfillment of the wedding feast?

The beginning point is pastoral leadership. Pastors must stop avoiding biblical texts with eschatological themes. When the first Sunday of Advent rolls around, go ahead and deal with the little apocalypse in Mark 13. If you are uncomfortable with such biblical texts as Daniel 7, 1 Thessalonians 4, or Revelation 5, reequip yourself in interpretation and exegesis. Read new material on apocalyptic material and homiletics such as *Preaching Apocalyptic Texts* by Larry Paul Jones and Jerry L. Sumney (Chalice Press). Identify your biases and aversions. Go ahead, include these texts in your preaching schedule. While you are at it, teach a short elective course with a name like *Contemporary Christians Reading Baffling Scriptures: Making Sense of the Biblical Future.*

Make use of Advent to revisit the power of nonapocalyptic prophetic texts. Listen to the voices of pre-exilic and exilic prophets and their longing for restoration and homecoming. Allow airtime for Isaiah, Jeremiah, and Ezekiel. Listen to the later Christian voices as they rediscover earlier Hebrew texts for a new hope:

> Every valley shall be lifted up,
>   and every mountain and hill be made low;
> the uneven ground shall become level,
>   and the rough places a plain.
> Then the glory of the LORD shall be revealed,
>   and all people shall see it together,
>   for the mouth of the LORD has spoken.
>
>   (Isa. 40:4–5)

What images come to mind immediately? Roads, paths, wide expanses leading toward the unknown horizon? The yellow-brick road that ultimately leads to restoration and home?

In addition to homiletical moves, allow the whole liturgy to look forward. In Advent, the serial lighting of candles already moves us forward toward the fulfillment of time. Imagine, if you will, however, how key themes included in worship bulletins, on posters outside worship areas, or projected on screens could simply redirect our eyes from preoccupation with the fleeting present to the wide expanses of the future:

> Eternity Now and Then
> How Far Is the Future?
> Waiting, Watching, Wondering
> Incoming God!
> Silence Takes Time
> The Answer Is Yet to Be
> God Creates the Future

Alternatively, think not in words, but in images. What montage of poems, photos, or sculpture might capture the sense of such profound words as "faith is the assurance of things hoped for," "no eye has seen, nor ear heard," or "we see now through a darkened glass, but then we shall see face to face"? Could it be a photo taken from inside a darkened room as a partially opened door reveals the hidden brightness outside? The sculpture of a gnarled hand reaching upward in desperation? Or a piece of poetry such as the following from poet laureate Seamus Heaney's *The Cure of Troy: A Version of Sophocles' Philoctetes:*

> History says, *Don't hope*
> *On this side of the grave.*
> But then, once in a lifetime
> The longed for tidal wave
> Of justice can rise up,
> And hope and history rhyme.

In the end, the biblical narrative itself will lead us toward the future of God—*if we will but listen to it.* The stories of the witnesses of scripture point toward the unknown horizon of God, a journey in which we are accompanied by One whom we seek. It is urgent and daring business, this kind of spirit travel. Listen! I tell you a mystery: we shall all be changed! In a moment, in the twinkling of an eye, at the sound of the last trumpet (1 Cor. 15:51–52). Catch your breath. Or sing to the heavens. Or keep silence before the mystery of it all. Whatever you do, it's coming.

In the same way that the biblical story leads from creation to fulfillment, from Eden to the new heaven and earth of Revelation 21, so the future always returns to the beginning. The turning of all time is found in the life of God, and eternity envelopes everything that passes through it. Or, as T.S. Eliot puts it so well:

> What we call the beginning is often the end
> And to make an end is to make a beginning.
> The end is where we start from.
>
> "Little Gidding," from *Four Quartets*

At its best, transforming worship does exactly this. It is a beginning that is an end from where we started. From it we may praise the God of all time, launching to the depths and plunging toward the future, living in the sacred space found between what was and will be. In the middle of it all, the community of faith may be transformed into the beloved of God.

> O God, our help in ages past,
> our hope for years to come,
> be thou our guide while life shall last,
> and our eternal home!
>
> Isaac Watts, 1719

Sources

Baptism, Eucharist, and Ministry. Faith and Order Paper No. 111. Geneva: World Council of Churches, 1982.

Bell, Catherine. *Ritual Theory, Ritual Practice.* New York: Oxford University Press, 1992.

Best, Thomas, and Dagmar Heller. *Eucharistic Worship in Ecumenical Contexts.* Geneva: WCC Publications, 1998.

Bradshaw, Paul, Cheslyn Jones, Geoffrey Wainwright, and Edward Yarnold. *The Study of the Liturgy.* New York: Oxford University Press, 1992.

Carson, Timothy. *Liminal Reality and Transformational Power.* New York: University Press of America, 1997.

Crossan, John Dominic. *The Historical Jesus: The Life of a Mediterranean Jewish Peasant.* San Francisco: HarperSanFrancisco, 1991.

Dix, Gregory. *The Shape of the Liturgy.* Westminster, Eng.: Dacre Press, 1944.

Driver, Tom. *The Magic of Ritual.* San Francisco: HarperSanFrancisco, 1991.

Eliade, Mircea. *Rites and Symbols of Initiation.* New York: Harper Bros., 1958.

Longley, Michael. *Bjorn's Pictures,* in *Signals: An Anthology of Poetry & Prose,* ed. Adrian Rice. Newry, Northern Ireland: Abbey Press, 1997.

Placher, William. *Unapologetic Theology.* Louisville: Westminster/John Knox Press, 1989.

Polk, David. *On the Way to God.* Lanham, Md.: University Press of America, 1989.

Sample, Tex. *The Spectacle of Worship in a Wired World: Electronic Culture and the Gathered People of God.* Nashville: Abingdon Press, 1998.

Thompson, Bard. *Liturgies of the Western Church.* Philadelphia: Fortress Press, 1961.

Turner, Victor. *The Ritual Process: Structure and Anti-Structure.* Chicago: Aldine, 1969.

Webber, Robert. *Worship Old and New.* Grand Rapids, Mich.: Zondervan, 1994.

White, James F. *Introduction to Christian Worship.* 3d ed. Nashville: Abingdon Press, 2001.

Wren, Brian. *Praying Twice.* Louisville: Westminster John Knox Press, 2000.